# Structure of Human Life

# Structure of Human Life
# A Vitalist Ontology

MICHAEL A. WEINSTEIN

New York University Press
New York *and* London

**Library of Congress Cataloging in Publication Data**

Weinstein, Michael A
  Structure of human life.

  Includes bibliographical references and index.
  1. Ontology.  2. Vitalism.  I. Title.
BD311.W44        147        79-2304
ISBN 0-8147-9189-1

Manufactured in the United States of America

TO GORE VIDAL
A Defender of Finite Life

# CONTENTS

# FOREWORD

The philosophy which is introduced in the following pages might best be called by the name "critical vitalism." Its roots are in the philosophies of life that arose at the turn of the twentieth century in response to the stalemate between idealism and positivism, but it is critical in its adoption of twentieth-century strictures against metaphysical speculation. My "recurrences" to the turn-of-the-century thinkers are recorded in the Afterword to this book. The essence of vitalism is partisanship in favor of life. For the classical vitalists, especially Henri Bergson, the defense of life took the form of the metaphysical postulation of an *élan vital* or vital impetus at the heart of being. A process of continuous change was thought to undergird and make less fundamental the discontinuities of ordinary experience. A critical vitalism restricts attention to the evidence provided by life grasped from within a body, by a particular organism or self. This evidence gives no support for the hypothesis of an eternal creative process but reveals embodied experience to be composed of conflicting tendencies which are incapable of final reconciliation. Life grasped from within is finite, but in its fusion with awareness it has infinite pretensions. The continuity which Bergson sought to equate with primordial being is betrayed by stubborn limits revealed in each durational moment. Critical vitalism, then, is a defense of our contradicted being, which is essentially polemical and disharmonious, seeking the impossible goal of completing consciousness.

A vindication of life as it is, with all of its tensions, must be made against death, its great enemy. In the realm of philosophic discourse death's greatest representative is the mysticism of the void, in which sheer awareness, the nothing, is made primary over the living body, grasped in its limitations. Vitalism and, in particular, critical vitalism, is at the opposite pole from the mysticism of the void, but it appreciates this mysticism as the purest and most honest expression of resignation and denial. The vitalist has no argument with the mystic. The first has chosen to try to affirm the finite and the second has chosen to try to affirm the limitless. The vitalist does have an objection against those who purchase their resignation cheaply by devising symbolic substitutes for vivid, immediate, and ultimate completion. Western philosophy, which Alfred North Whitehead called a series of footnotes to Plato, has been predominantly occupied with devising such symbolic substitutes ever since Plato fused knowledge and purpose in the "idea of the good." The contradictory idea of the conscious completion of life is the response of critical vitalism to Platonism. All symbolic harmonies which are thought to reveal the essence of being result from the "cognitive fallacy" of replacing life with meaning. To center one's life around a meaning which arises out of that life and which represents but a fragment of it is to deliver oneself to the inert, to make of life a practice for death.

Finite, embodied life needs a defense, although commitment to it is beyond justification, because we are beings divided between Eros and Thanatos. My defense of ourselves against ourselves is undertaken by describing the major possibilities and motives of a life grasped without symbolic completions and harmonies. There is a structure or order to these possibilities and motives, which is why the general title of the discussion is "the structure of life." The subtitle, "a vitalist ontology," should be understood to mean a critical examination and defense of our being as it is lived from within. My ontological presumption, then, is that our being is lived being and is known to be such through awareness, which is other than life. The ontology, then, is dualistic and the synthesis of life and awareness is left uninterpreted. I address the discussion to beings who are discrete selves and who can decide their fundamental attitudes toward existence in radical separation from others, but who can also be receptive to appeals. I wish to heighten both the separation and the receptivity, put them into tension with one another, and thereby make life more vivid and true to itself.

I have been aided in this project by Dr. Deena Weinstein of DePaul University, who contributed to its every stage of development, Dr. Francisco J. Moreno of New York University, whose concept of basic fear, developed in his work *Between Reason and Faith,* is essential to my discussion of desire and fear, Dr. Helmut Loiskandl of the University of Queensland, a wise friend, and Ms. Despina Papazoglou of New York University Press, who expertly shepherded the manuscript through to publication. I also thank the Rockefeller Foundation for granting me its Humanities Fellowship in 1976, during which time much of the planning and outlining of this work was done.

# CHAPTER I

# SKETCHES OF OUR BEING

A work of philosophy is neither a novel nor a drama, although it may borrow its form of expression from literature equally as well as from science. The primary feature distinguishing philosophy from literature is that the former must strive to eliminate mystery, whereas the latter thrives upon it. Philosophy should present its conclusions at the beginning and then show how it reached them. Literature, though it uses foreshadowing, suppresses the fullness of its meaning until the last word has been written. Philosophy has no secrets because it seeks, always unsuccessfully, to transcend time, which always has surprises in store for us. The very essence of literature is insistent temporality and therefore surprise.

I will begin my discussion of our existence, then, with its conclusion. We are beings who express one another to ourselves. Our deepest essence is not intercommunication but intracommunication. Each one of us takes the suggestions, hints, complaints, and assurances of others and absorbs or rejects them through interior dialogue and strife.

We are thoroughly representative beings, yet we also have a uniquely personal and irreplaceable core. We achieve our freedom in a struggle for and against others, not by separation from them. But let there be no mistake. We are capable of extreme singularity in which we return to the source of our awareness in the boundless infinity of nothing. In contrast, mysticism demonstrates only our dependence upon others. Without others, even if they do no more than haunt our memories, we are nothing. As Ortega y Gasset wrote in his mature work, *our* life is the radical reality.

The notion that our essence is to express one another to ourselves (that only superficially do we express ourselves to one another) overturns our ordinary understandings about ourselves. We have learned many bad lessons over the centuries, the most important of which are that knowledge can make us good and that our essence is to be independent and autonomous. These two lessons go together, because it is the truth that is supposed to make us free. Very few have dared to tell the deeper truth that an adequate cognition is a pale substitute for a rich life and that we free one another through our fortitude and forbearance. We flee desperately from the terrible insight that goodness is encompassed by trust and loyalty toward beings who are as finite, corruptible, imperfect, and incomplete as we know ourselves to be. We are, perhaps, incapable of living by and for this deeper truth. We are frightened and we panic when we let it be revealed to us, and then we seek refuge in the world of material objects or in the realm of spirit. We seize upon anything that can be interposed between ourselves and others.

I understand philosophy to be the guardian of the deeper truth about our being. A philosopher should stand, without compromise, between myth and science, warning us against the siren songs of our own creations. The standard of philosophy is free and responsible criticism of our life as a whole, so it cannot be based on either the final causes of myth or on the efficient causes of science. Both final causes and efficient causes are intelligible refuges for beings who are subjectively and objectively insecure. We cannot get along without them in everyday life, but perhaps we can slowly learn to acknowledge them for the conventions that they are. Philosophy is a vindication of ourselves, not as we wish we might be, but as we are. We may find comfort in the belief that our aspirations will be necessarily fulfilled or even that they certainly will not, but philosophy must declare that such opinions are groundless. Philosophy exacts the sacrifice of myth but gives freedom from blind determination in return.

There is no starting point for a philosophy of our existence but that existence itself, filled with all of the interpretations of it. Philosophy must get by with the single presupposition of free criticism, the truth of which cannot objectively be demonstrated. Critical freedom implies an effort to understand ourselves, to take an ironical stance toward any interpretation of our existence, and to assault any definition that we give to ourselves. It aims at uncovering hidden motives, desires, interests, and fears. Critical freedom also implies letting a self that has agonized over its meaning speak for itself about its deepest experiences.

## 1. METHOD

The aim of philosophy, at least as I understand it, is to leave us without any recourse but one another. There would be no philosophy, then, were it not for our proclivity to devise barriers that separate ourselves from each other. The origins of these barriers, their structure, and the thesis that they are not merely the results of cognitive errors will be explored as this discussion proceeds. There is a vast difference between a philosophy in the process of formation and one that has reached its basic conclusion. A philosophy that is being created is never clear about its own method, because a method can be systematized only in retrospect. We define the pattern our thought has taken when that pattern is complete. Therefore, any attempt to reproduce the history of a philosophical creation is pretentious and undertaken in bad faith. A critical description of existence is achieved only after a long series of false starts, many passages up blind alleys, and bouts of frustration and disillusionment. The method by which the final conclusions were reached becomes apparent only when the starts have been understood to be false, the alleys not to be open-ended avenues, and the frustration and disillusionment to be overcome. The systematized method represents the procedure that would have been followed had the conclusion been known in advance.

The method by which I have concluded that we express one another to ourselves is what Miguel de Unamuno called "agonic doubting." Unamuno contrasted the provisional and methodical doubt of René Descartes to his own agonized questioning of his existence. Cartesian doubt suspends belief only to ground it later on in self-evident and certain first principles. Descartes allowed himself the luxury of doubting the world but paid the price of remaining self-confident. His confidence, of course, did not run very deep, because he had to buttress it with his provisional morality requiring obedience to convention and authority. He purchased freedom of thought at the cost of a responsible life. There was nothing provisional and methodical about Unamuno's doubt. He subjected himself to the most brutal self-inquisition, pushing himself to reveal the secret that his ideals were merely veils concealing his abject hunger for immortality. Unamuno even doubted his own doubting, arguing at times that it might be fraudulent or, alternatively, that he should have kept his secret. Unamuno, then, doubted his very existence, his motives, and the ideas that gave him comfort. He plunged to what he called "the bottom of the abyss" where he found nothing. He struggled upward in order to affirm the tragedy of a life without rewards, rationalizations, or excuses. If Descartes gazed into the abyss, he did not tell us about it.

Agonized doubting is personal. It begins with the troubling insight that I may not be who I tell myself that I am. It impels me to challenge my self-definitions, to consider that others may interpret me more adequately than I interpret myself, to acknowledge that I may not be conscious of my motives, and to scrutinize my dreams, fantasies, obsessions, and fears for signs of meaning that I have suppressed. For each one who undertakes it, agonized doubting reveals a unique autobiography rich with particular personal relations and historical encounters. But it also discloses a structure of existence that sustains each unique autobiography. This structure is the object of philosophy. Agonized doubting opens up subjective insecurity and brings forth the person.

## 2. SKETCHES OF OUR BEING

The structure of our existence is complex and heterogeneous, and therefore it cannot be described adequately by means of any single image or definition. The task of description is made no easier by the fact that whatever unity characterizes us is not only mental but sentimental and volitional. The various symbols through which we approach our existence are at once bound to each other and autonomous, in harmony with each other and in conflict. Images and definitions are included within our existence, but paradoxically they stand over it and presume to regulate and control it. They are exclusive of one another, whereas our existence is inclusive of all of them. The following are merely preliminary sketches of our being, each one showing an aspect of our existence that is revealed by agonized doubting and free criticism. At the outset of our inquiry we shall see ourselves as polemical, incomplete, and durational beings.

The method of agonized doubting both implies and is appropriate to polemical beings who are struggling against themselves and one another. Conflict between human beings and between the groups into which they are organized is a commonplace fact of ordinary life, but such observable strife is not often traced to its interior origins. A close inspection of experience shows, however, that the apparent unity of consciousness is a fragile synthesis of warring parties, each of which strives to gain supremacy over thought and action. Just as in the state, where disputes are compromised, dissent repressed, and revolutions plotted and executed, the very structure of the person is political, not so much mirroring the public situation as grounding it. The treaties and truces that make up law, the mechanisms of control that maintain biased orders, and the ideologies that legitimate domination are bloodless reflections of the betrayals, suppressions, and lies by which we keep up a semblance of personal continuity. It is no less difficult to keep peace within the self than it is to maintain political order. It is as much a mistake to believe that the tenuous practical unity of a person is more basic than passional division as it is to maintain that official justifications adequately describe the public situation.

Henri Bergson acknowledged the polemical structure of human existence when he wrote that the self is composed of mutually compatible and mutually contradictory forces. On one side he identified the "fundamental self," bursting forth with novel content continuously and yet mysteriously remaining intimately linked to its past. Opposed but necessary to the fundamental self was the "conventional ego," whose function was to assure a conceptual continuity of personality over clock time. Fundamental self and conventional ego could not help but be at war with one another. The first would seek to express its immediate and fresh response to the world actively, while the second would censor this response to make it conform to an abstract plan. Bergson indicated that the conventional ego resulted necessarily from "the requirements of social life," but he did not explain what he meant in detail. In one respect, the present discussion is intended to elaborate on his hint.

Bergson's tragic vision of the self, in which the more primordial and spontaneous force is inexorably denied full expression of itself, is intrinsically political. The fundamental self is the party of change and the conventional ego the party of order. It is absurd for us to take sides in this deepest of disputes, although it is probably inevitable that we become partisans. Only one who was entirely the prisoner of fear could support the conventional ego unequivocally. Such support would deny the existence of the fundamental self altogether, and spontaneity would be repressed or named in deceptively familiar terms. One who sought to get along without the conventional ego would have to be either a suicide with no care for self-preservation or a saint with no destructive impulses. The fundamental self is beyond good and evil; it is capable of any judgment, always according to the circumstances. Perhaps Bergson's colleague, William James, was the wisest when he counseled that the apparent self be made as liberal, inclusive, and appreciative as possible. Yet even James acknowledged the inevitability of sacrifices and either/or choices.

The division that Bergson discovered at the root of human existence can be characterized as a split between expression and control. Bergson based his conclusions on what he called "intuition," which involved an effort to "invert" our ordinary "practical viewpoint" and attend to experience as it appears. The results of intuition should not be accepted on faith, and Bergson urged others to attempt his experiment. Having followed his advice, I find, just as he did, that we are divided into mutually complementary and mutually antagonistic selves. One of them, which I call expressive rather than fundamental, responds with a total commitment to each passing event, investing that event with emotion and crying out to unite with it or destroy it. The expressive response is neither sporadic nor chaotic, but is a judgment on experience, bringing to bear upon the event an autobiography. Expression is not mute but is the molten flow of speech out of which languages congeal. Expression is centripetal, personalizing experience according to emotion and drive. Opposed to expression is control, always calculating costs and benefits, and ever ruled by fear, especially the deep fear that conscious unity may at any moment be dissolved. Control is the principle of the conventional ego, exerting the centrifugal force that is watchful for danger. It exacts the sacrifice of personality to assure the maintenance of individual identity.

Unamuno, another of the early vitalists, insisted that the study of consciousness be supplanted by the analysis of intraconsciousness. As did Bergson and James, Unamuno severed "the man of flesh and bone" into person and individual, and then set the two at war. The person was the "principle of continuity" through time sustained by contributions to others, while the individual was the "principle of unity" in space, maintained by possessions. Unamuno thus transferred the conflict between fundamental self and conventional ego to the practical realm, pitting generosity and charity against greed and fear. Unamuno's existence, as he describes it poetically in his *Tragic Sense of Life,* was a continual polemic between person and individual. The demand for "all or nothing" was the cry for an absurd synthesis in which he would be both himself and everyone else. Unamuno recognized the absurdity of his demand, but he believed that its very impossibility liberated him from finite terrors and freed him to affirm life.

As polemical beings, political animals to the core, we are fated never to achieve peace and harmony. Partisans of order may urge us to trim our desires, dampen down our passions, and alleviate our anxiety so that we can adjust to others' expectations for us, but we achieve synthesis only by surrendering appreciation of life's complexity. Promises that we can be ourselves and also be at peace with ourselves are delusive and conceal an impulse to tame, domesticate, and dominate us. Other deceptive enchantments are offered by those who counsel us to flee from our inner turmoil to the service of an impersonal ideal or a collective meaning. Advocates of change, who urge us to dispense with convention, care nothing about our fragility and are purposefully ignorant of our fear. We have nothing to carry us from one day to the next but those conventional certitudes that bind us to others. Yet we inevitably and fortunately rebel against them. The partisans of order dwell in fear, while those of change are so terrified that they overlook it. We are not destined to any harmonies but those born of privation. Plentitude presupposes conflict.

The polemical vision of our existence results from vitalistic intuition, which removes practical self-restraint and reveals the sacrifices that we make to appear to be whole. Another interpretation of our being does not seek to get behind practice but to analyze it. What Bergson called the "practical viewpoint" is the synthesis of expression and control, the first providing the end and motive, and the second the norm and procedure. The ground of action is negation, privation, and want; the paradoxical experience of lacking something, which creates the future by drawing us into it. To be indigent is the hallmark of living; in fact, if we attend closely to our distinctions we find that we differentiate the living from the dead by the category of want. A creative negation seems to support the luxuriant growth of living things. Want impels living organisms to seek their completion, their nourishment, their ecological niche. Of course, this is life interpreted only anthropomorphically.

Chemists tell us that the living and the dead shade off into one another at the margins and that they are distinguished by different chemical reactions. We know differently about ourselves because we live from the inside out, feeling the stimulus of desire give us vitality and the stimulus of fear deaden us. In our more poetic moments we believe that it must be the same for all living beings and, perhaps, for the world as a whole.

The practical viewpoint, which is life's stronghold, shows us that we are not so much polemical as incomplete. Life, at least as it is manifest in us, is never satisfied and evinces the insatiable will that so tormented Arthur Schopenhauer. The mistake of vitalist metaphysics was to maintain that we are goaded or driven by life. But how can we be impelled by what we are? We are intrinsically goading and driving beings who are capable, as Friedrich Nietzsche observed, of mendacity. The lie here is to believe that somehow life is a problem set before us. Certainly we are more than alive. The cool awareness that attends Bergsonian intuition transcends vitality. But that awareness is hideously impersonal. If we are anything we are living. If we take ourselves to be pure attention we are, indeed, as the Buddhists teach, nothing.

To be an incomplete being is primarily to want. Considered as an experience, wanting is indescribable. We find it impossible to speak about an absence except by making it appear to be something present. Rather than speaking of want as such, we say that we "have" one or another want, as though we possessed something. Yet we do not possess primordial want as much as we are possessed by it. Just as we devise ideal harmonies to conceal the strife at the core of our being, we cover over our felt indigence by convincing ourselves that we own needs, feel desires, or entertain possibilities. We may even go so far as to claim that one of these needs, desires, or possibilities is more fundamental than the others, and that if it were satisfied we would be complete. But with regard to life's viewpoint, Martin Heidegger was correct in stating that care ends only when we draw back from the world and die. Care is the practical response to the yawning want that constitutes our life.

On the far side of intuition, beyond spontaneous expression, we spend our days in pursuit of meaning. Each desire that has not been satisfied, each unmet need, each possibility that has not been actualized spawns a substitute ideal that represents it. For the most part, we do not live within the richness and complexity of the undivided present but toward a future only vaguely prefigured by a symbolized ideal. Each action that we undertake promises more at its inception than it can deliver to us. Action itself, whatever its object may be, is exclusive, narrowing our attention from all that might satisfy us to a particular aim, which we tend to fetishize for the moment. Once we are done with our task, however, want reasserts itself, and we seek to busy ourselves once again with something else. Repeated frustration, which is our destiny, may impel us to mistake symbolic for concrete fulfillments. We are capable of living by and for ideals, either sacrificing our unique existence to them or withdrawing from activity and dwelling among them. Ultimate meanings, at least, provide symbolic completion, but just because they are not concretely present we strive to assert them dogmatically and make others believe in them.

The only ideal that is not deceptive, the native ideal of practice, is the conscious completion of life, which implies the absence of want, the richness of experience, and the presence of awareness. We cannot conceive of life's ideal intellectually because awareness is a function of want, which divides us from our experience and transforms that experience into circumstances. The very idea of change is not primordial but presupposes an effort to achieve some fulfillment. We cannot imagine being aware of stasis. Life's ideal, then, is paradoxical, mirroring life's contradiction. Life is necessitous, mendicant, incomplete, and unresolved. Yet these very characteristics imply their opposites of liberation, richness, completion, and resolution. But were life to be fulfilled, at least from a practical viewpoint, it would cease. The native ideal of life hearks back to the plentitude of the womb, with the additional demand that plentitude be conscious. Critical philosophy can merely note the contradiction within this ideal and reveal our indigent essence. Religions speak to our hopes, but they are ruled by mystery.

When we direct ourselves to the present, through intuition, we find that we are polemical beings, divided by warring selves. When we attend to our future in our practical lives, we discover that our essence is to be incomplete. Only the past remains to provide a third sketch of our being. When we try to determine who we are, our only resource is what we have been. We are historical beings in the strictest sense, ever coordinating disparate experiences into a temporal unity that we call character or personality. Character is an achievement of human existence, whether or not it measures up to conventional moral standards. It is not given to us before we emerge into the world but is the product of the expressive responses that we have succeeded in carrying forth into action. When we transform an appreciation of life into a deed that appreciation becomes actual and forms a piece of our autobiography. We are then able to reflect upon its consequences and decide whether to repeat it or to reject it. Each lesson that we learn from being-in-the-world is engraved upon our memory and creates a personal tradition that may either sustain us or imprison us. Reflection upon the past shows us that we are concrete beings, irreducibly particular and continually mutating. Unamuno captured our concretion and particularity in his notion that each one of us is a unique species. Character is not unified by a plan but a sequence of related personalities, each one melting into the next. Sometimes the continuity seems to be broken by a crisis, in which we must choose to advance or perish, but in the midst of such a crisis our past is brought forward to secure the resolution.

Unamuno, who based his thought about human existence on the concrete "man of flesh and bone," was preoccupied with our historical being. He distinguished between the official histories by which leaders legitimate their rule and mobilize their followers, and intrahistory, the past of a people made present in its traditions. Official histories are practical, providing meanings for the future by fabricating a usable past. Intrahistory supports practice just because it is taken for granted and is not the object of calculated manipulation. The same distinction holds within each one of us. For practical purposes we give ourselves meanings and then ransack our pasts in order to anchor them. Meanwhile, beneath the rhetorical turmoil, we change, often imperceptibly, in response to new events. We never fully appreciate the unique beings that we have become, because life insists upon throwing us back into the abyss of want. We seek the universal, the certain meaning, the adequate and timeless cognition, because we crave security.

But in our infinitely complex particularity we are greater than any of our self-definitions.

From the viewpoint of rational analysis, we all share certain common characteristics, such as the need for nourishment and the certainty of death. But from the inside we are united by our differences. As Josiah Royce put it, we are individuated by contrast effects. Each one becomes a person by qualitative differentiation from others. The notion that each one of us is an intrinsically unique autobiography runs against our ordinary and practical understanding of society, which seeks to interpret everything, including ourselves, as instruments to an impossible completion. For the economic order we are factors of production, performing tasks that others might do more efficiently. For the political order we are legal fictions, invested with abstract rights and duties that may transcend our lifetimes. Only when we stop to appreciate ourselves and others do we realize that behind the expedient society of functions and fictions is a society of concrete persons, none of whom can be substituted for any other. Of course, each one of us cooperates in maintaining the conventional delusion. We are necessitous beings who are dependent upon one another, and one side of us insists that others be predictable machines. The price of others fulfilling our expectations is that we mechanize ourselves.

Regardless of economic and political imperatives, however, we are, in Ortega's words, irreplaceable and insubstitutable. The horrifying gulf between the painfully intense intimacy that we are to ourselves and the dimensionless shadow world of everyday social interaction points to the deepest tragedy of our common life. Only by extreme self-forgetfulness do we bring ourselves to believe that the fundamental distinctions among persons are moral. Each one of us, as even the benign Gabriel Marcel admits, is beyond good and evil in the recesses of intimacy. A uniquely particular being cannot be judged, at least primordially, according to moral rules. Not even Nietzsche was able to touch the core of our concrete durational being, which mutates, complexifies, creates, maintains, and destroys its own traditions whether it is hopeful or despairing, courageous or cowardly, self-assertive or self-effacing. If we may speak at all of a supreme intrinsic value, it is that our richness be brought forth and manifested in our deeds. Yet we are practical beings who are vulnerable to fear. We can liberate ourselves only within restricted confines and depend upon others to free us through trust, loyalty, and forgiveness. Fear, which is merely want turned back upon itself, is the agent of expediency and the creator of calculation. Were we to overcome fear, we would acknowledge our uniqueness. But we are unique to ourselves only in retrospection. Toward the future we are incomplete, and in the present we are at war.

The three sketches of our being as polemical, incomplete, and concrete are merely provisional, constituting primarily an introduction to the temperament, mood, or sensibility of the following discussion. From each one of these descriptions can be drawn the observation that we are beings whose overriding relation to ourselves is one of disguise. In the present we convince ourselves that we are harmonious and equilibrated when we are really at war. Toward the future we tell ourselves that we might (or will!) complete our meanings when our only meaning is to struggle for an impossible resolution of our contradicted life. Retrospectively, we give ourselves a definition, a self-concept, when we are actually so unique that no definition exhausts our appreciation and expression of experience. We cannot help but put on these disguises and, if "ought" implies "can," we should not attempt to do without them. Our disguises are not cognitive errors but result, in a way that we cannot comprehend, from fear. How fear, the supreme negation of life, is able to generate a kaleidoscope of substitutes for living is a problem that encompasses the being of consciousness. A philosopher should not dare to struggle with this problem, because only myth can speak to it. Philosophy can teach us what tragedy is and, perhaps, prepare us to live with the most acute awareness of which we are capable. If it encroaches upon the territory of myth, it is doomed to dissolve in the acid of self-criticism or to falsify itself by joining the agents of miracle, mystery, and authority.

### 3. LIFE AND AWARENESS

Each of the sketches of our being presupposes a description of the elementary components that make our existence possible. Put in another, more technical way, an ontology, or an account of the modes of our being and their relation, grounds the images of our being. The ontology to be introduced here and elaborated upon in the remainder of the discussion is dualistic, reflecting the polemical and tragic character of our existence. This ontology is the outcome of an analysis of the evidence revealed by intuition, which shows that we are syntheses or composites of fundamentally heterogeneous elements. In summary statement, we are uneasy, tenuous, and fragile compounds of life and awareness. From the viewpoint of life we are conscious animals, transforming awareness into intelligence, which is an instrument primarily of survival in its many forms. From the standpoint of awareness we are incarnated spirits seeking liberation from our contingency and our temporal bounds. When neither life nor awareness is supreme over the other, we are free beings who check and balance life's ruthless insistence with appreciative compassion.

The word "life" here is used in the vitalistic, not the scientific, sense to designate the dynamic that we intuit from the inside when we release ourselves from concern for the achievement of particular goals. As I have noted in the foregoing sketch of incomplete being, the essence of life is want, a negation that we cannot describe positively, but that somehow is also what Bergson called a creative impetus. At the heart of life, then, is a union of opposites that we cannot explain intellelctually but that we describe mythically through stories about creation. Science is indifferent or repugnant to vitalistic intuition, pursuing the project of treating life according to the categories of death. Yet mechanical aggregation and combination, the principle of efficient causes, is merely the most effective instrument of intelligence, which itself is a projection of the vital process. Science presupposes objectification and abstraction, both of which are late syntheses of polemical, incomplete, and concrete beings striving to anchor themselves securely in the world. Considered intuitively, mechanism is derived from vitality, functioning as a tool of practical existence. The irony of life is that one of its functions, intelligence, constructs interpretations that deprive it of its own being. From the naturalistic viewpoint of science, dead matter preceded the emergence of life by eons and will continue long after life has perished. According to this interpretation, life itself is simply a more complicated type of mechanical process. Yet we do not live as we believe machines work.

Life, as we experience it, is inexorably dependent upon that which lies beyond it. It is primordially judgmental, dividing, as George Santayana observed, circumstances into dominations that threaten it and powers that sustain it. Life is particularized, oblivious to universal truth, careless about any ultimate significance it might have, and protective of its own special niche. It is also individualized by, and expressed in, an organism, the external sign of its contingency, frailty, and finitude. Life is the synthesis of the functions that relate it to its circumstances, including, for human beings, sensation and, even more important, gesture and vocalization. The principle of life is merely expression of its powers, whatever those may be. All attempts to impose a norm upon life—for example, survival—result from reflective viewpoints that already presuppose the synthesis between life and awareness. We do not know the meaning of life because we do not know the powers that it may evince. We have some inkling of the limits of our own lives because we are concrete beings with autobiographies.

We experience life with a minimum of awareness as William James's "blooming and buzzing confusion," for which there are no sharp demarcations between the internal and the external, subject and object, means and end, but only an impulsion onward. Most often our encounters with life in the raw are not delightful interludes but terrible crises. There are times when our elaborate plans collapse and we lose our orientation; we must make a decision, but our grounds have dissolved and we panic. Everything spins around in a meaningless whirl of quality to which we react chaotically and with ever increasing horror as we lose our grip. We lose, in Paul Tillich's terms, our "centeredness," which requires a decent alienation from life. Whatever life in the raw may be for animals coordinated by instinct, it is a chamber of horrors, worse than a nightmare, for human beings.

At the opposite pole from life is awareness or attention, that mode of our being which makes us cognizant of life and allows us to halt the flux of sensation and the insistence of volition long enough to grasp its structure. While life is radically personal and particular, attention is impersonal and universal. Its province is not a realm of ideas separate from, and constitutive of, life, but life itself in all of its complexity. If we are able, though deceptively, to speak about life scientifically, attention eludes the formulas of intelligence altogether. Awareness is a mute bystander to all that we feel, think, and do, performing the single function of saving the fleeting present so that we can have what we call experiences, durational unities that nonetheless are fated to melt away.

Even more than life, attention is the subject of myth. The greatest modern myths, the philosophies of absolute idealism, attempted to ground reality in awareness, accomplishing the feat of making the perfectly transparent opaque by endowing it with thought and meaning. But thought is merely an uneasy synthesis of life with awareness, the means by which life captures awareness. Were we to put it mythically we might say that life, enchanted by the peace of the unbroken present held in attention, attempts to retrieve that present by inventing symbolic unities of thought. The deep synthesis of awareness and life is expression, the fundamental self. The more superficial synthesis is the conventional ego, ruled by the motive of control through meaning. We cannot explain the presence of attention. It seems to be eternal, yet in our lives it comes and goes. We may opine, without any proof but an analysis of our experience, that when the powers of life are developed and integrated to a certain point they create a dwelling for awareness. As life ebbs awareness flees from it, only to return when it is confident enough to flow once again. Were we to construct an evolutionary myth, we would say that life's purpose is to make itself a proper dwelling for awareness, which in and of itself is diffuse, impersonal, and unlimited. Perhaps this is what Heidegger meant when he taught us that our vocation is to make a clearing for Being.

The fact that awareness is sporadic in our lives, that it is always inadequate, that it never holds more than a minute portion of experience and even that for only a moment, shows the frailty and provisional character of our existence. From our own ideal viewpoint, from which we reflect upon perfection, we are trial copies and failed experiments of a being who would resolutely grip experience attentively, never falling away from it, never reducing it to a game, never inventing symbolic consolations for it. One of critical philosophy's cruelest lessons is that we live in and for truth only when we acknowledge our radical insufficiency. Awareness is never capable of holding the richness of life, and life is never able to capture the boundlessness of attention. We will not and, indeed, cannot live in and for truth, which again indicates that knowledge is not virtue.

There are times, cherished by the mystics, in which life seems to fall away from us or, better, in which attention appears to recede from life, carrying us with it. Experience then is a veil of illusion. Sight is two-dimensional and objects fade into one another; sound is distant and hollow; touch is detached from our inwardness; smell and taste are absent. Unlike the other extreme, in which we are immersed in life and desperately struggle to act, mysticism stills volition. With the deadening of will goes the dispersion of conventions, plans, and projects, which are revealed to be mere practical expedients. As we withdraw further and further into our intimacy, we are drawn into the impersonal void of pure attention, isolated from all relations. This is Nothingness, which, for all who have known it, exerts a terrifying fascination. The mystics dare to court the void, to marry themselves to their destiny, to cherish the vacant universal that suffuses us. But for a partisan of our existence mysticism is the greatest sin of pride, tempting us away from our finite, but concrete, lives and, most important, dissolving our loyalty to others and our trust in their care. We are compounds of life and awareness, and if we honor ourselves (and there is no necessity for us to do so), we must walk on a knife edge between want and its renunciation.

Life and awarness are never present to us in their purity but are inferred from the evidence revealed to us when we journey to the limits of consciousness. Only mythically do we account for ourselves in terms of them, although the persistence of myth indicates a wisdom in us that refuses to allow us to believe that we are the grounds of our own existence. What we call human lies between the two elements that compose us, both of which tenaciously resist explanation in our own terms. Life and awareness are neither subjective nor objective but are the grounds of the synthetic unity of existence out of which subject and object are differentiated for both action and appreciation, the two primary modes of our being. The following discussion will be based on the fundamental duality of our being but will refer to it only from the viewpoint of our centeredness as polemical, incomplete, and concrete beings. We will not venture any more on the terrain of ontology, which is too dangerously close to myth's preserve.

## 4. POLARITIES OF BEING

The notion that our being is a synthesis or coordination of life and awareness can be further described and illustrated by reviewing and reinterpreting several of the polarities that have been the subjects of much philosophical discourse. These polarities, such as the finite and the infinite, relatedness and nothingness, desire and fear, pleasure and pain, and analysis and synthesis, cannot be neatly ranged under the heads of life and awareness. Some are related to aspects of the two primary modes of being, others to their synthesis in our existence. Also, the list of polarities is not exhaustive but is intended merely to be illustrative. Our existence cannot be systematized according to the kind of geometrical pattern envisioned by Baruch Spinoza; and an adequate description of it must be flexible, allowing for loose ends and a certain imprecision.

The traditional distinction that is perhaps most closely related to the split between life and awareness is that between the finite and the infinite. Sören Kierkegaard based his philosophy of existence on the proposition that our being is a mysterious synthesis of finitude and infinity. Nikolai Berdyaev held the same thesis, distinguishing further between the "bad" or "false" infinite of abstract intelligence and the genuine infinity designated often by the word "eternity" and identified here with pure attention.

Edmund Husserl insisted upon differentiating the infinite task of truth seeking from finite and contingent inclinations, and specific historical circumstances. We could trace the importance of the distinction between finitude and infinity for contemporary philosophy back to Immanuel Kant's antinomies, although the analysis in *The Critique of Pure Reason* is confined to scientific knowledge and does not touch upon our concrete existence.

In relation to the primary polarity of life and awareness, individuated life is finite and awareness infinite. Life's finite character is disclosed not only by death itself but much more by such presentiments of death as dependency, contingency, and limitation. Our radical dependency upon others, circumstances, and our own creations is probably the most overwhelming and significant characteristic of our life. We all acknowledge this dependency, at least in practice, but we flee from facing up to its full implications. Few, if any, doubt that their existence could be sustained without nourishment, aid, and care from others, as well as cultural objects; but just as few allow this certainty to guide the conduct and interpretation of their lives. We tend to seek independence desperately through the narrowness of individual or group egoisms and even more through absolute deliverance to God or to some superpersonal meaning that turns our attention away from mundane dependencies. Philosophers help us in our flight by sapping dependency of its existential import and reinterpreting it as determination. Determinations can be observed and noted scientifically, leaving us with the specious notion that we might gain control over them definitively. Unreasoning faith in technology is a sign that even in the popular mind determination has been substituted for dependency. But determination is merely a deprived or, in Heidegger's terminology, a "privative mode" of dependency. Full realization of one's dependency is a terrifying experience that reveals that whatever one knows or does, one's own efforts will never be sufficient to sustain existence. Recognition of dependency demands an existential and unreasoned choice between trust in what we already know is unreliable and suspicion. The partisans of technology have implicitly chosen suspicion, banking on the triumph of knowledge over life.

Dependency is at the root of our contingency and limitation. While from a retrospective viewpoint we may be uniquely concrete, we cannot know ourselves to be uniquely necessary within any scheme of efficient or final causation. We are born and we die at particular dates, encountering and assimilating circumstances that we did not create, and leaving most of our capacities unused, work unfinished, and contributions lost. What we do, think, and feel are contingent upon particular opportunities, themselves contingent upon deeds and circumstances that can never be exhaustively traced down. We, of course, flee from acknowledging our contingency by surrendering ourselves to systems of meaning that make our lives necessary, because belief in necessity deadens awareness of our limitations and our responsibility to choose within their boundaries. The dogmatical "true believer" and the anarchist pursuing boundless possibility have in common a resentment against life's restriction, which they disguise by glorifying abstract freedom. Neither the "positive" freedom of comporting oneself in accordance with necessity nor the "negative" freedom of doing as one wishes confronts the issue of resolute decision within a web of particular dependencies.

Life's finitude is in polar opposition to the infinity of awareness. Although awareness that has found a dwelling in life is sporadic and radically limited, it is, in principle, boundless and capable, we think, of comprehending ever more of life's complexity. The great mistake of those who honor awareness more than life is to believe that its infinite potential is or might be made actual. But life is inherently finite, and awareness without life, at least so far as we can know, is vacant. Awareness, as has been noted, is merely a bystander. Life does all the work and attention follows it, when conditions are propitious, as did a James Boswell pursuing a Samuel Johnson. Were we to speak mythically, we might opine that awareness was somehow able to give life its animation through a breath of spirit or, alternatively, that life spontaneously generated its companion; but neither dualistic nor monistic metaphysics stands up to philosophical criticism, which remains indifferent before either hypothesis. A philosophy committed to vindicating our existence as it is can counsel only that we struggle to increase our span of attention to the maximum so as to appreciate as much as possible our finitude, particularly as it is expressed by our dependency.

Closely bound to the polarity of finitude and infinity is that of relatedness and nothingness. Life is inextricably related to that which lies beyond it and may even be said to be exhausted by those relations. This is merely a more positive way of stating life's dependent character. From a static and reflexive standpoint, we know our dependency; from the practical viewpoint of action, we find ourselves to be related to the world in all of its dimensions, physical, social, and cultural. Every new relation that we integrate into our existence deepens, enriches, and makes more complex our life, while every relation that we lose kills us. When we provisionally dissolve our relations through a meditative discipline, we have a foretaste of death, which is not a meaningless nihilation but a withdrawal into the nothingness of attention. I take it that this is what Heidegger means when he tells us that death is a nonrelational possibility, our ownmost possibility. Acknowledgement of our being-toward-death, according to Heidegger, "individualizes" us and frees us to make resolute choices within the confines of our mundane finitude. Nothingness, then, is the condition of that distance from life which allows us to exist as polemical, incomplete, and concrete beings. Recognition of the nonrelational possibility provokes the deepest existential choice of all, the choice between affirmation of life as it is and rejection of life. Affirmation demands acceptance of one's particular relations, not as morally or practically justified, but as a basis for conduct. Rejection involves, either actual destruction or that symbolic destruction that delivers one to a superpersonal meaning, principle, or ideal. The affirmation of life is intimately bound to trust in the beings on whom we are dependent; rejection of life is the active partner of suspicion.

A second set of polarities cuts across those of finitude-infinity and relatedness-nothingness. Desire and fear, pleasure and pain define the tensions that we experience as syntheses or compounds of life and awareness. Both desire and fear are forms of want that have been interpreted and made the basis of practice. Desire is life on the move, reaching out to capture, assimilate, and enjoy that which lies beyond it, whereas fear is life turned back upon itself, seeking to exclude or destroy what is alien and threatening to it. In its purest form, desire is supremely confident and careless, trusting in its fulfillment and enamored of its object. It is the force of Eros, worshiped by Plato and Sigmund Freud, that forges and sustains relations. Desire is not hopeful but secure in itself. Hope appears only as a response to fear and frustration and indicates a judgment that one's own powers are insufficient. Desire is not selfish but is, paradoxically, disinterested. It does not calculate its probabilities of success or seek to control its circumstances but simply moves to unite itself to its object without concern for consequences. Desire is rooted in the lived and expanded present, and so it does not concern itself with the organism's good over a long term.

Most philosophers have denigrated desire because it leads us to immerse ourselves in perishable enjoyments, particularly those of the flesh, which often bring disease, injury, or at least discomfort in their train. Yet without desire's bold, blind, and naive confidence we would lose our intimate bond with the world. The exuberance of sexual vitality, even when it borders on lust; a hearty appetite, even when it exceeds itself in gluttony; a passion for movement, even when it becomes reckless—all insert us more firmly into existence than any project, plan, ideal, or faith. We are doomed to betrayal by desire because we are essentially mendicant and divided, but love's bitter harvest need not make us dishonor its fecundity.

Desire seems to arise from within ourselves, constituting the conscious expression of what Freud called "libido." It is not necessarily selective about its objects but will seize upon any number of occasions to gratify itself. Selectivity or connoisseurship, like hope, arises as a consequence of betrayal and indicates an underlying fear of frustration or disappointment. Intelligence, which makes distinctions among objects according to their consequences (dominations and powers), is not the perfection of life, but, as Bergson and Max Scheler noted, a sign of its failure to ramify spontaneously. The ideal standards that guide the connoisseur's selection are responses to fear, just as are the engineer's practical criteria. Desire's native optimism is primordial in our existence, but we almost never experience it in its fullness because very early in our lives we become the prisoners of fear.

The polar opposite of desire is not aversion, as Thomas Hobbes thought, but fear. As was noted above, fear is inverted want, desire turned back upon itself. Fear is the conscious expression of life frustrated by its dependency, contingency, and limitations. Desire is personal but not private. It includes its object within itself and seeks to unite itself to it. Fear, in contrast, individualizes by making us aware of ourselves as distinct entities who are threatened by what lies beyond our control. In its most elementary form, fear is particularized, impelling us to ward off specific dangers so that we can maintain ourselves as we are. Repeated frustration and exposure to threat, however, can generalize fear to the point that we are governed by an overall policy of suspicion and distrust. Rampant fear can lead us in the two opposite directions of withdrawal from engagement in our circumstances and aggressive attempts to control them (suicide and murder, asceticism and instrumentalism, despair and faith).

Although fear is not primordial in our existence, it is essential to it. Self-awareness, which is often thought to be the mark of our distinction from other animals, is probably the consequence of fear and betrayal. Philosophers have disguised this terrible possibility by restricting fear to its most privative mode, cognitive doubt. The occasion for cognitive doubt is our basic insecurity in the world. Despite our practical expedients, we know that our circumstances are unreliable, that whatever their ultimate value may be, they proximally contain dominations as well as powers. Descartes understood this, though imperfectly, when he identified thinking with doubting. His formula, "I think therefore I am," should be modified to read, "I doubt therefore I am," and, even more fundamentally, "I fear therefore I am." The fallacy of Descartes and, more generally, of most Western philosophy has been to restrict fear to doubt and then to claim that cognitive certainty is the goal of thought and, by implication, of life. We might call this mistake the cognitive fallacy and insist that it is not merely an intellectual error but the hallmark of inauthentic existence. The cognitive fallacy is expressed practically by the principle that knowledge is virtue. Yet no knowledge, not even the deepest self-knowledge secured through agonized doubting and intuition, can still our essential fear. Knowledge can offer only symbolic compensations for fear (faith and hope) or expedients for eliminating or controlling the objects of certain fears (technology). Authentic existence does not involve knowledge of true principles but a struggle to overcome fear despite knowledge that fear makes the struggle possible by giving us our individuality.

Fears of external threats arising from the objective insecurity of our existence are accompanied by an even more profound and basic fear rooted in subjective insecurity.

Fear of our circumstances leads us to control thought, feeling, and will, or, to put it in the terms of psychiatry, to repress our desires. The tenuous unity we create through self-control is ever in danger of being shattered by desires, compromises, and betrayals we have allowed or forced ourselves to forget. Thus, we become fearful, not only of what lies beyond us, but of ourselves. Our distrust and suspicion of others is mirrored by an intimate insecurity. A critical psychiatry would describe all of the mechanisms by which we disguise fear of ourselves by fear of others and our circumstances and, alternatively, how we disguise external fears by fear of ourselves. Memory, which is the ground of our unique and concrete being, is also the curse that haunts our conventional self-definitions.

Fear, which gives us individuality, has the further consequence of isolating us. The price we pay for being uniquely concrete is an essential solitude that terrorizes us. This solitude is most evident at the extremes of our existence, when the synthesis of life and awareness is about to break apart and we are on the verge of being plunged into life or drawn back into the void. At such times we are acutely aware that we are alone, that only an existential affirmation can sustain us. This affirmation of our polemical, incomplete, and concrete being overcomes fear and centers us once again in the world and among others. It does not, however, banish fear, which immediately begins to suffuse experience, requiring repetitions of the existential decision over and over again. Existential decision, of course, can be evaded or short-circuited by any number of symbolic compensations that conceal our solitude. Among such compensations are deliverance to God, identification with a group, concern about loneliness (rather than solitude), and pursuit of philosophy or any other cultural endeavor as a consolation for living.

For nineteenth-century utilitarian psychologies the object of desire was pleasure and that of aversion pain. In the present discussion this linkage is not made. Following the revolt against psychologism that occurred at the turn of the twentieth century and was exemplified in Husserl's phenomenology and G. E. Moore's intuitionism, the object of an interest is distinguished from the experience that accompanies its satisfaction or frustration. Pleasure here is considered as the whole experience in which a desire is united adequately and satisfactorily with its object; pain is defined as the sensory signal of frustration or of diminution of life. Hence, pleasure and pain are not symmetrical. Pleasure is an aspect of life's dynamism, fulfilling an impulse that emerges from within, whereas pain may be altogether extrinsic to the organism's vital direction.

Pleasure never appears as an isolated feeling or sensation but is always an aspect of an activity that creates an expanded and structured present. The structure of pleasure is dramatic, each pleasurable activity constituting a history of its own. The paradigm case of pleasurable experience is fulfilled sexual activity, which involves arousal of a desire, tension toward union, and release of tension and separation. It is noteworthy that sexual satisfaction is social and is achieved only in propitious circumstances. Other more private pleasures also involve tension and release but are less dependent on an appropriate context and do not involve as much of our character and capabilities in their satisfaction. Every pleasure, however, is a synthesis of heterogeneous qualities in a temporal unity. Even aesthetic appreciation, which many philosophers believe is disinterested, occurs only when attention is awakened and fear is stilled by an apparent harmony. As attention is drawn to the aesthetic object we deepen our vicarious participation in its perfection to the point at which our involvement becomes so exclusive that other impulses, extrinsic to appreciative contemplation, assert themselves and disperse awareness.

The structure of pleasure reveals our finitude, dependency, contingency, and limitation. Although a desire that integrates our energies and moves harmoniously toward its fulfillment is the most favorable occasion for attention to capture an undivided present, the expanded and lived present is always, from our practical viewpoint, brief and fleeting. We cannot imagine perfection but can conceive of it only in contradictory terms, because all pleasures essentially contain release and separation. All pleasures exclude many of our capabilities, and no pleasure can unite us to the totality of our circumstances. Yet our native ideal, the conscious and total satisfaction of life, can be defined as an undivided, continuing, and pleasurable present. We have nostalgia for the comfort of the womb but not sufficient nostalgia to still our demand for awareness. We can be satisfied ultimately only by intimate synthesis with a greater life than our own, but it must be a synthesis in which we do not sacrifice our individuality. From the standpoint of our polemical, incomplete, and unique being, life's native ideal is unintelligible. This ideal, however, is the ground of the existential affirmation of life. It is the only ideal that is not a symbolic compensation for failure, because it is not possible to live for it, only by it. Pleasure, then, is the essential ideal, the ideal that is immanent to life, not transcendent over it.

While pleasure unites us to its object and opens up an expanded present, pain isolates us and drives us out of the present and into the future, impelling us to seek relief. Pleasure synthesizes and coordinates experienced wholes, whereas pain breaks them down and makes us dwell on particular objects and sensations. Pleasure is complex and kaleidoscopic; pain is monotonous and instantaneous. Pleasure carries the past within it into the present activity. Pain, in contrast, drives us to ransack the past for expedients that might alleviate it. Pain is intimately bound to fear and thus may be the most profound cause of our individuality. Were it not true that we necessarily suffer pain, we would, perhaps, never exist as individuals in the divided time of past-present-future, plotting, planning, calculating, and projecting; preserving our integrity.

Those who equate pleasure and pain, dividing circumstances into positive and negative stimuli or reinforcements, necessarily deprive pleasure of its complexity and drama and make it into a kind of negative pain. Pleasure as we experience it, however, is spontaneous and inclusive and cannot be analyzed into specific data. The reduction of pleasure to pain, particularly by behaviorists, indicates suspicion and distrust of life expressed as a boundless will to control and regulate by simplification. Each of us is, indeed, in the grip of fear and at the mercy of pain, but our vocation is to affirm our condition as it is, not to embroider it with the delusions of myth or pseudoscience. Our elemental choice is between affirming life in its uniqueness and incompletion and reacting against life through dedicating ourselves to symbolic substitutes for it.

The last polarity of our being to be sketched here is that of analysis and synthesis. If philosophy is free and responsible criticism of our life as a whole it must be analytic, investigating and describing the components of our fragile unity and how they relate to one another. Although the primary terms, life and awareness, result from intuition, they cannot be discussed without defining them conceptually. Discourse about concepts, however, is ruled by the law of noncontradiction. The polemical structure of our existence, then, appears to involve logical contradictions when we elucidate it. We can overcome the resulting unintelligibility only imperfectly, by resorting to such deceptive formulations as "mutually antagonistic and mutually compatible selves." These formulations do not provide knowledge of objects that can guide practical endeavors but are, at best, invitations to agonized doubting and personal exploration of experience. Analysis can deflate the pretensions of myth and science, but it cannot replace their certitudes with new ones. Critical philosophy opens the way for existential choice, but its denial that knowledge is virtue prevents it from doing any more.

The analytical procedure of philosophy contrasts sharply with the synthetic unities of experience that we spontaneously apprehend in our encounters with our circumstances. While for the intellect particular events and objects are interpreted as instances or examples of concepts, in our concrete life specificity and particularity are the criteria of reality. What is most real for us is not that which is most cognitively certain but that which we cannot mistake for anything else. From a scientific viewpoint the real is the interchangeable. Science attempts to break synthetic and qualitative unities down into elementary components, which are then recombined according to mathematical functions. The prestige of science derives from the fact that the entities it discovers, postulates, and puts into relation can be correlated with perceived phenomena in everyday life. Manipulations of those entities provoke predictable changes in phenomenal unities, and so science has impressive practical efficacy. Yet our native viewpoint is not practical but appreciative. Our practical life is grounded, as Ortega noted, in sets of uniquely interrelated circumstances. Our particular life is the radical reality within which scientific inquiry and technological projects are rooted.

Whether or not our judgments are metaphysically defensible, we tend to deem most real those contexts and objects that are most familiar to us and to which we are related in the richest and most complex ways. Those objects and circumstances that we have brought into our ken, that we repeatedly encounter, that have been assimilated into our lives—that, in brief, provide partial completion for our restless will—stand out among others as unmistakable and therefore as real. The basic conservatism of life, which counterbalances its novelty and adventure, is a result of our need to orient ourselves to particular circumstances, which then become familiar and serve as implicit standards for judging anything else. It is relatively easy to transfer technologies from one culture to another because their effective use is indifferent to specific configurations of quality, but it is much more difficult to export social institutions. The use of a tool requires training to perform a restricted set of movements, while dwelling within an institution demands a sentimental and volitional education.

The reality that is most unmistakable to us is another person with whom we share our lives and upon whom we are dependent for completion. We are able to relate to the other person in more and richer ways than to any other aspect of our circumstances. But the difference between persons and the other objects in our circumstances is not merely one of degree but also one of kind. The objects we encounter are surrounded by an environment that affects them, but persons are the centers of circumstances they interpret and then attempt to transform, preserve, or destroy. The incompletion of each person adds an element of risk and trust to social relations, calling forth a dimension of freedom that is absent in our other encounters. Our relations with other persons are not merely extensively complex, as they are with familiar objects with which we have repeated encounters, but are intensively complex because they necessarily change in response to transformations in the others' interpretations of themselves and of us. The absolutely unique and mutating presence of the other person is our most profound criterion of reality, but it is a standard that cannot be defined intellectually because it cannot be interpreted in conceptual terms. Insofar as fear impels us to try to control other persons, our attention is diverted from their particularity and they lose reality for us, becoming unreliable instruments to our goals. In our practical lives analysis rules, driving us toward the abstract entities of science. In our appreciative existence we spontaneously apprehend syntheses, the paradigm for which is the other person.

## 5. ANTECEDENTS

The critical purpose of philosophy requires personal responsibility for inquiry and for the conclusions that follow from it. Nobody who attempts to present a critical portrayal of our existence can accept in advance the first premises of another thinker and then merely endeavor to sort out their logical implications. However, the philosopher's responsibility does not require even methodological naiveté about the work of predecessors. By the time one has achieved the confidence to undertake independent reflection, one has already created a perspective from which to interpret existence, the content of which includes judgments that have been made by others. If I am correct that we are beings who express one another to ourselves, most of any philosopher's interpretation of existence is composed of other's thought and experience. Philosophy cannot be pursued in a cultural vacuum, not only because of its obvious dependence upon dialogue, but also because free criticism often overturns the practical certitudes that provide us with a sense of security. Philosophers are notoriously suspect by society, but they are also suspicious of themselves. Were it not for inspiring examples in the past, it would be very difficult to cut one's moorings to everyday practical life and to criticize oneself and one's circumstances.

The present discussion does not follow in the path marked out by any specific contemporary school of thought but draws inspiration from particular thinkers who undertook similar critical projects and often disagreed among themselves profoundly. Bergson, James, Unamuno, Nietzsche, and Santayana, all of whom have contributed to the perspective developed here, had in common the project of vindicating our existence against both what Unamuno called the "inquisition of science" and the dogmatic historical faiths of idealism and its derivatives. Each of them found in the process of life itself, grasped from within, the basis for comprehensive philosophical reflection. They did not interpret life from the standpoint of biological science but examined it as it appeared to them in its immediacy. Bergson's élan vital, James's "will to believe," Unamuno's "hunger for immortality," Nietzsche's "will to power," and Santayana's "primal will" are all expressions of life's nisus toward conscious completion. These terms are not abstract concepts summarizing the universal characteristics of being but are names referring to the inner dynamism of existence.

The vitalistic tendency of thought, which the thinkers named above represent, first emerged in the nineteenth century in response to biological evolutionism and in reaction against metaphysical idealism. The category of life was intended to provide a critical synthesis of scientific mechanism and historical teleology. Early vitalism was flawed by an attempt to interpret life as a metaphysical absolute, which led many thinkers, particularly Bergson, to affirm irrationalist doctrines. The vitalists' irrationalism, however, was never as comprehensive as their critics made it out to be. The vitalists, for the most part, confined themselves to critiquing what was called above the cognitive fallacy. They were insistent in proclaiming life's spontaneity, paradoxes, uniqueness, and unpredictability against all attempts to explain its meaning or purpose intellectually. They did not despise the intellect but gave it a limited and practical function within life. They taught that the intellect is not an organ of creation but one of control. They did not deny the necessity of control but strove to elucidate the sacrifices it involved.

As against most interpretations, I believe that the early vitalists were citics in the Kantian sense of that term. They struggled against both the dogmas of idealism and mechanistic skepticism to vindicate each person as an end. Bergson's effort to mediate between mechanistic and finalistic biologies, James's attempt to walk the tightrope between tough-minded science and tender-minded theology, and Unamuno's passionate polemic between reason and life all reveal a Kantian project of holding the middle ground of human existence against our own efforts to destroy it and hence to destroy ourselves. This project of defending ourselves from ourselves, which I take to be the essence of Kant's philosophical revolution, must be repeated in every generation, because superhuman dogmatism and infrahuman skepticism will continue to reappear as long as human beings exist. Both are responses to our constitutional dependency and fragility, which provokes a fear of living. Each time we reduce ourselves to the outcomes of efficient causes or deliver ourselves to the service of an ideal we diminish our lives in order to gain a specious security. Living in the human dimension demands that we open ourselves to the full range of our possibilities, not only the powers but also the dominations. That we never adequately meet this demand is a result of our essential frailty, and philosophers should be generous enough to refrain from legislating imperatives and confine themselves to offering invitations. The early vitalists, certainly, were not adequate to the demands of a critical life, but at least they had the courage to explore realms of experience that are neglected by science and sublimated and domesticated by myth. They often suffered severely for their efforts, experiencing depression, agony, and repeated crises, all of which invariably result from courting the void. But they persistently affirmed life, even after experiencing its limits, and it is in this affirmation, rather than in any of their conclusions, that they inspire me.

## 6. MOTIVES OF EXISTENCE

The previous discussion has presented a provisional and introductory sketch of the primary elements of our existence and their relation to one another and to the living synthesis that we directly experience. Our existence has been interpreted as polemical, incomplete, and concrete; and these images have been grounded in the basic polarity of life and awareness. Other polarities—finitude and infinity, relatedness and nothingness, desire and fear, pleasure and pain, analysis and synthesis—have been linked to the primary existential division, and the entire inquiry has been placed in the context of vitalistic philosophy and its methods of agonic doubting and intuition. The purpose of this chapter has been to prepare the way for a discussion of the fundamental motives of our existence, the signs under which it is possible for us to live. However, before even initiating an examination of our motives it has been necessary to critique the cognitive fallacy, the notion that an adequate cognition can provide a principle to guide the conduct of life. Our motives are open to critical reflection, but I have argued that rational criticism cannot substitute for the intrinsic struggle of existence to overcome the fear that is essential to it.

Each of the motives of existence is intimately bound to

the struggle against fear. The motive of control, by which we ordinarily live, is derived from the attempt to overcome fear and dependency by mastering, taming, and domesticating the self and circumstances. Control involves making life safe and secure by simplifying it and reducing its variety to monotony. In external relations it is expressed in the drives for property, power, deference, and corroboration. In the internal relations of the self to itself it is expressed by the restrictions of the conventional ego. The motive of control is based on the understanding that dependency can be overcome only through mutual fear. Society is interpreted, at best, as a defensive alliance, in which each one restrains the others from endangering the security of all.

The motive of appreciation arises when we temporarily surrender our fear and allow others and ourselves to appear to us as we are, as polemical, incomplete, and concrete beings. While control is ruthless, spoliating the possible, appreciation is compassionate, sympathizing with all expressions of life and seeking to capture in attention their sentimental and volitional quality. Appreciation reveals the fundamental self in its particularity and pities the inherent failure of life. While control divides us from one another, recombining us only through the expedients of economic functions and legal fictions, appreciation unites us to one another through insight into our specific and intimately personal dependencies. Appreciation dreams of a society in which each one completes the others by acknowledging their uniqueness and alleviating their fears. Yet the appreciative viewpoint is acutely aware that practical life will always defraud its vision.

The motive of sacrifice is the dialectical synthesis of control and appreciation. It acknowledges both the fear that drives us to make all things, including ourselves, instruments, but it also carries forward appreciation's insight that we will never achieve by our own resourcefulness a completion of our lives. Sacrifice stands between control and appreciation, grounding itself neither on success nor on pity but on risk, trust, and fidelity. Its aim is neither security nor sympathy but bringing forth into action relations that minimize control and maximize the expression of each particular life. Sacrifice is elusive, always fleeing either to the pursuit of a limited goal or to compassionate resignation. Its primary manifestation is not positive but is the silent act of according trust and loyalty to others, which may later be expressed actively by care and attention for them. The three motives of existence are our fundamental possibilities, but sacrifice is the only one through which we become lucid to ourselves.

# CHAPTER II

# CONTROL

Jean Jacques Rousseau remarked that we are born free yet are everywhere in chains. He did not believe that he could explain our predicament but attempted instead to demonstrate how it could be made legitimate. That we must be imprisoned, that we in fact willingly put ourselves in bondage is one of the first principles of any sound political philosophy. But with equal or even greater ardor we strive to smash our manacles and liberate ourselves from restrictions and limitations, especially those we have forged on our own. Our imprisonment, then, is always legitimate from one viewpoint and never legitimate from another. We may attempt to distinguish among better and worse prisons; this seems to have been the primary task of political philosophy since Plato wrote *The Republic*. But all prisons are expedients, and none will ever be commodious enough to contain the fundamental self. Most of our social life is consumed by efforts to place ourselves and others under control and then to overthrow the controls we have so painstakingly constructed. Control itself is essential, willed by each of us, but nonetheless it is intolerable. All particular controls are contingent, accidental, and provisional. Our contradictory attitude toward control is merely an implication of our polemical, incomplete, and concrete being.

## 1. THE PRINCIPLE OF CONTROL

Control is our active and practical response to our radical dependency upon what lies beyond our life. From every side our tenuous unity is vulnerable to dissolution or collapse from present threats, the repressed desires and traumas that haunt our memories, and the future consequences of our own and others' acts. We respond to our precarious condition by continual efforts to ward off dangers and to prevent their appearance through anticipation and cunning. Most often we are not even aware that we are trying to control ourselves and our circumstances. Our condition is so profoundly threatening that conscious existence is, for the most part, totally given over to the motive of control. Only infrequently, if at all, do we inhibit the motive of control long enough to become aware of how pervasive it is. We believe that animals are imperfect forms of life because they are delivered over to the biological cycle of nourishment, procreation, and nurturance. But we have our own cycle of self-maintenance, which, though it is more complex than the animal's failed struggle for equilibrium, is equally exigent.

In our everyday lives we are most cognizant of our attempts to control when we self-consciously plot a course of action with a limited goal in advance of undertaking the deed. The case of instrumentally rational conduct is so obvious and striking that we tend to think of it as a paradigm for all of practice. Yet instrumental reason is merely a sophisticated variant of the ubiquitous and less orderly process of control that shapes our existence even when we seem to be the slaves of passion or superstition. Just as some philosophers have interpreted our root insecurity as cogni-

tive doubt, ignoring our existential dependency and contingency, others have narrowed the concept of control to
include only instrumental reason, relegating the rest of our
conduct to the spheres of affectivity and faith. Most of our
efforts at control, however, do not involve the calculation
of ordered series of means to ends, but are arbitrary and
even self-destructive from an economic viewpoint. One of
the most important modes of control is the very selection of
some goals out of the many that are possible, and such
selection is certainly not instrumentally rational. Further,
the immanent ideal of life, its own conscious completion, is
unattainable, and therefore practice itself cannot be rationalized. Finally, just because we are continually controlling ourselves and our circumstances, we are not necessarily
doing so effectively in terms of anyone's interest or even in
terms of any interest at all.

Control, then, is not another word for the principle of
economy, which teaches maximum advantage with minimum effort. Control sinks so deeply into our life that we
may find that we restrict and limit ourselves in ways that
run counter to what we consciously believe is our own best
interest. Attempts to preserve the principle of economy, as
Freud did, against our obvious rebellions against it, by
postulating an unconscious compensatory economy, merely
read sophistication into experiences that are essentially in-
determinate in a teleological sense. The motive of control
originates in fear, which is perhaps the agent most corro-
sive of reason. In order to engage in the rational calculation
of consequences we need strong doses of confidence and
hope, which are available only when we have overcome
fear through nonrational devices and processes.

The most elementary meaning of control is restriction

and limitation. As dependent and contingent beings, we are severely limited regardless of what we do, but we are insufficiently limited to constitute a unity of experience. The functioning of our biological organsim is dependent upon a multitude of conditions, which modern science has impressively listed in detail. However, these conditions do not take care of themselves and are not ordered in such a way that they provide us with objective security. We must attempt to restrict our circumstances beyond their given limitation so that the powers are released and the dominations suppressed. The work of external control might proceed with ease were we well adapted to practicality. But the opposite is the case. Before we can even think of mastering circumstances we must have achieved a sufficient domination over ourselves to suppress the yawning want that lies at our core. Our primordial restriction of ourselves is the transformation of overwhelming want into separate and specific desires. Self-control, at least in our own particular lives, is prior, both temporally and logically, to practical control over circumstances. In fact, the basis of self-control, which is deferral of desire impelled by fear, is the ground of calculation, of hope, and therefore of practicality. The scientist who honors what is rather than what might be desirable is a pale reflection of the child who is watchful for the proper moment to make a demand.

The root of control is not in anything positive we might hope to accomplish but in the flight from our essential solitude, from the vacancy in which we may be left at any moment. The principle of control is that we should be fit to maintain relations with others primarily and to our non-human circumstances secondarily, that we never be left alone with ourselves. We are intrinsically social beings, not only in the sense that we need one another's aid to survive biologically, but in the deeper sense that our individual encounter with our circumstances is derived from our relations to others. Josiah Royce noted that the world is not primordially given to us as an object but is essentially the ground that lies between each of us and that mediates our relations to one another. Our initial orientation is to those who care for us and who can and do withdraw that care or substitute harm for it. Anthropomorphic interpretations of existence have the advantage over rational philosophies because they appeal to our primordial relatedness to persons. Through most of history human beings have made a remarkable effort to bring the world under control by personalizing it and appealing to it. In modern times this effort has been reversed, and today many seek to control others by depersonalizing them and treating them as utensils, manipulating them. Yet were the modern project to be carried out successfully, we would, indeed, be abandoned to our solitude and delivered over to a war of all against all.

We are threatened at one pole of our being by the blooming and buzzing confusion of raw life and at the other by the nothingness of attention. We hold ourselves on the knife edge between chaos and vacancy primarily through the force of convention. Symbols, especially in the forms of commandments, warnings, and encouragements, control us from within by providing us with vicarious completion and, just as important, with excuses for resolute action. We become human beings at the moment that we begin to legislate for ourselves. Our polemical being, which is revealed by intuition, is ordinarily disguised by a welter of rules representing temporary victories over desire and guaranteed by sovereign fear. The conventional ego, which is

merely an individualized legal system, is the combined police force, judge, and jailor that disciplines spontaneous
expression, and it is the military service that guards the
frontier with the abyss. We are delivered over to control,
are everywhere in chains, because we cannot help but
judge ourselves and then mete out the appropriate rewards
and punishments. The conventional ego is, of course, no
more successful in maintaining a peaceful and harmonious
order than is any other political system.

In the West the traditional strategy of political philosophy has been to define human nature and then to show how
the state might be brought into accord with our requirements. Yet by an almost strict analogy each one of us is a
state or at least a petty principality. Each one of us is a
concrete being with a distinctive personal tradition and a
set of customs, conventions, and laws that reflect it. Just as
a political regime may be arbitrary, repressive, and self-
defeating, so a conventional ego may tyrannize over life
and lead it from one disaster to the next. If we are unique
species, each with a history and a plurality of selves, we
must continually work to achieve unity where the underlying tendency is dispersive. Our nature is inherently political, and as such it cannot be used as the basis for resolving
the conflicts that occur in the wider polity. Plato was perhaps the only political philosopher who understood that the
self is political. The idea that the state is the individual writ
large abolishes any separation between politics and psychology. Human nature is not an Archimedean lever for
transforming society. Political and personal dynamics are
interchangeable.

Plato's insight into the reciprocity of politics and psychology was flawed by his commitment to the cognitive

fallacy. He believed that knowledge might make us virtuous by defining a possible harmony of the soul that could be translated into a just political order. For an adequate understanding of the substance of politics we must turn to that other great initiator, Hobbes, who taught that in order for the state to exist there must be a sovereign containing the war of all against all. The conventional ego is our own intimate sovereign, just as subject to the contingencies of circumstance and the burdens of history as is any regime. Our intimate sovereign is no wiser than our desires and fears allow us to be, and its power is limited by our continual rebellions against it. Control, then, cannot be rationalized, because reason is not the essence of our life but merely one of its functions. From the viewpoint of control, life's immanent ideal of conscious completion is the Hobbesian ceaseless search for power after power. The conventional ego cannot abolish this search but can temporarily suppress some of its expressions and, more important, divert it through deception into channels that are acceptable to others or that are relatively harmless to continued existence. The principle of control, which is merely to maintain a tenuous conscious unity over time, does not order the good life. At best, it organizes enough of life's dynamism to allay fear by holding out hopes, bribing desires, defrauding life, and most important, by substituting symbolic fears for real ones.

## 2. THE DYNAMICS OF FEAR

One of the commonplaces of our existence that we tend to forget when we have a grip on ourselves and our circumstances is how easily harmony, peace, and confidence can be dissolved. We may, for example, be thinking beautiful and splendid thoughts about a desired good when suddenly we feel a sharp pain and our attention flees from the ideal to the immediate threat to our security. Or we may be sharing a moment of union with another and find it destroyed and negated by words betraying doubt, mistrust, and selfishness. Fear is the universal solvent of desire and pleasure, poised to overflow the boundaries of hope and faith that we have constructed for it. Our moments of perfection, equanimity, and disinterested alertness are achievements that indicate that we have overcome fear temporarily. Desire may precede fear temporally, but once we have become separate individuals fear is prior to any other aspect of our active life.

Fear withers, contracts, and immobilizes life, leading us to retreat into ourselves and to tremble at what we are. Were we to live fearlessly, we would plunge ourselves into each realm of experience, enjoying and suffering all that it had to offer to us and expressing its felt relation to us. Our special vocation would be the artist's, to personalize existence, to respond to appearance by placing the stamp of our attitudes and moods upon it, and to order our sentiments into unities that might be shared with others. We would affirm who we are unequivocally, thoughtless and careless of our individual destinies. Yet we live not only to bring life to expression but to extend life into a self-created time.

We are capable of expressing any experience directly but fear. Although in ordinary life we believe that fear's object is some particular threat that lies beyond our intimacy, careful scrutiny reveals that beneath all of the specific dangers is the pervasive fear that we are inadequate to our own existence. We are able to respond confidently to challenges to which we believe that we are equal or superior; in fact, we often welcome and court risk, so long as it is limited. But we are thrown into panic and terror when we can summon no resources to meet a situation and are left alone with our impotence. The child who screams for an absent parent, the adult who stands helplessly by while someone else resolves a dangerous situation, and the person whose plans have been unexpectedly defeated—all of them are thrown back upon their own incompletion. Indigence has no appropriate expression but a silent plea for aid and sustenance.

Once we have tasted fear we no longer express life innocently in each expanded present. Fear is the fruit of the tree of knowledge of good and evil, which separates us from our circumstances and from others and impels us to create the time of the symbolic past-present-future, in which we are condemned to work by the sweat of our brows, to bear children in pain, and to plan and calculate under the shadow of our dependency and ultimate death. The biblical account of the Fall contains the profound truth that we are not primordially moral, but expressive beings, whose task is to add conscious expression to the raw dynamic of life, to affirm by naming. When Santayana observed that we divide circumstances into dominations and powers, he was correct in making frustration prior to achievement. We learn about good and evil by experiencing evil and then attempting to overcome it through strenuous effort or symbolic substitution. Before we are exposed to the withering ray of fear we are innocent of comparative judgments. We allow life to follow its course, commenting upon its vicissitudes but not calculating its outcomes. Fear, by exposing our vulnerability and destroying our security, makes us selective and teaches us that we must have standards, that we must legislate, that we must rebel against appearance.

Fear is the sign of life's failure and insufficiency. So long as awareness is directed toward any aspect of life's dynamic it is filled with particular qualities held in tension. But when fear thrusts attention back upon life itself—when, in Heidegger's terminology, we attend to our being-in-the-world as such—we dwell in our own desolation. We find a lack, at the center of ourselves, an absence that must be filled if it is not to eat everything else away. There are many paths that we take to the acknowledgment that we are, as Heidegger said, the null basis of our own existence. Kierkegaard was shocked into awareness of his radical dependency by the agony of justification before God, Fëdor Dostoevski by the mystery of crime, Unamuno by the lack of any rational guarantee of immortality, Nietzsche by the failure of the will to power, and Jean-Paul Sartre by the nullity of freedom. We never lack the conditions for becoming aware of our fragility. Any fear that we do not immediately suppress can draw us back into the primordial fear.

Fear cannot be expressed directly and immediately because it is our response to privation, incompletion, indigence, and negativity, all of which refer to want. We express fear indirectly by all of our attempts to control our circumstances, others, and ourselves. The ways in which we control our circumstances and one another are familiar to us, but the more fundamental dynamics of self-control are usually hidden and function most effectively when we are not aware of them. The overwhelming motive that grounds our practical life is the desire to ward off fear, to find some excuse for carrying ourselves from one present into the next, to marshal our energies to surmount our basic impotence. Our variations on the theme of control are manifold, but each one has as its goal the fabrication of a conventional unity sufficient to impel us beyond our immediate situation.

The paradox of control is that it does not appear to us as a response to our indigence but as a drive to add to existence. We are most under control when we are sure of ourselves, confident about the future, and hopeful. When life seems most promising, when we are pleased the most with our efforts, and are aware most acutely of our capacities, we have temporarily succeeded in dispelling fear, creating a sense of security, endowing ourselves with meaning, and releasing some of our powers. We gain confidence, however, only by a prior act of restriction in which we limit the range of our possibilities and withdraw attention from the risks that any enterprise involves. Yet the achievement of confident security is precarious and subject to dangers that have been suppressed. Our transient unity rests upon definitions of ourselves and our work that we project into an essentially uncertain future. We never project all of what we are capable of expressing, nor do we acknowledge how arbitrary our selection of possibility has been. When our conventional unity begins to wear thin, as it must, we resort to more obvious methods of self-control, such as promises to reward ourselves if we sustain the effort to live, threats to punish ourselves if we do not accomplish our aim, and imaginative representations of the disasters that will occur if we give up. Less than anything else do we want to acknowledge that our unity is conventional and that our natural tendency is toward dispersion. Much of our conscious life, then, is a series of attempts to convince ourselves that we necessarily are what we have defined ourselves to be. We will to believe that we have obligations or have a destiny primarily so that we will not lose the self-image that mediates between our awareness and our fragile dependency.

All attempts to control others and circumstances presuppose the constitution of a self with sufficient unity to express a coherent set of desires and to calculate the probabilities of their satisfaction. The self in its form of the conventional ego functions as a buffer between what lies beyond intimacy and the spontaneous judgments of the fundamental self. The conventional ego is not given to us like one of our biological organs but is self-created in response to fear. It is expression's compromise with fear, resting upon submission to a sovereign of our own making. Our sovereign, of course, is no stronger or more competent than we are. If we are nurtured and cared for sympathetically when we are infants, our conventional ego will be able to draw upon a rich tradition of satisfaction that will make its rule more benign than it will be if we are subject to gratuitous privation and harm. If we have been encouraged to take risks, to express our desires, to learn how to surmount difficulties, and to make of frustration a challenge, our conventional ego will be flexible, generous, and subject to alteration. If we have been restricted and sheltered, our conventional ego will be repressive, exclusive, and vigilant. However, regardless of how favorable our circumstances may be, we will never be free from fear and thus will always have to control ourselves on pain of losing our conscious unity.

### 3. CARE AND ATTENTION

Before we become aware of our dependence upon physical circumstances we understand our bonds to other human beings. Our situation as infants, which is prolonged throughout our lives despite our efforts to disguise it, is that we exist on the sufferance of others. Before we care about our own existence and its meaning, we must be cared for and given meanings by others. Before we can attend to our circumstances, we must be accorded attention. We experience within ourselves life's dynamism, and we express that dynamism spontaneously. But we are not monads. We must be given partial completions to our being, and we must be taught to express ourselves coherently. Most certainly, these observations are commonplaces, but we frequently neglect to scrutinize their implications. Our stubborn dependence upon others for the very content of our conscious life mocks not only any metaphysical individualism but also any practical individualism. We are indeed unique, but each one of us is uniquely representative of others.

In relations among adult individuals a distinction is made between demand and appeal, justice and mercy. In the infant's cry there is no such differentiation but only a primordial call for help. The cry indistinguishably mixes assertiveness and helplessness and communicates nothing but dependency, contingency, and limitation. The infant calls forth the other blindly and is sometimes fortunate enough to receive a response. We return to infancy in those moments at which we break down in tears, alternately and simultaneously enraged at, and begging for, solace from another person. If we allow ourselves to cry in this way we recapture our original situation and are humbled by the frailty of our conventions. Of course, the motive of control conspires against such outbursts, diverting us constantly into building symbolic and material defenses against full acknowledgment of the grounds of our being.

Although moral wisdom may proclaim that it is better to give than to receive, our being is structured so that we must have received a great deal before we can give anything. Our dependence upon others is so vast that we can never contribute more to them than they have provided to us. Yet we rebel against humility before others and prefer to set ourselves over and against them or, even more perniciously, to humble ourselves before God or a great cause, because none of the gifts that we have received is adequate to the demands of our life. We notice that most of the care and attention accorded to us is not voluntary, that we can always be exiled, and that the others upon whom we stake our lives are unreliable. We learn not to cry but to demand whenever possible and to appeal when we have not been able to establish our rights. We attempt to insure continued care and attention by controlling our responses and by manipulating others.

"Care" and "attention" are special words that demarcate the vague and shifting boundaries between subject and object, thought and action, self and other. We care about others by sympathizing with their plight, attempting to understand them, and participating vicariously in their fulfillments and frustrations. We also provide them with care by ministering to their physical and emotional needs, warning them of dangers, and aiding them when they are helpless. Similarly, we attend to others both by listening to and observing them carefully and by serving them actively. We seek care and attention from others, particularly from those

with whom we are in immediate contact, and are disappointed when we do not receive them in their fullness. We
distrust those who care for, and attend to, us only in an
objective and active sense and who are indifferent or anti-
pathetic toward us emotionally, because we believe that
their aid is not based on an acknowledgment of our being
but on self-interest or on some abstract obligation. We
scorn those who merely appreciate us subjectively because
they fail to acknowledge our practical dependence upon
them. All human beings, not only children, need acknowledgment, aid, recognition, and solicitude in the full sense
that combines appreciation and action. When this need is
unmet and only the deprived forms of care and attention
are present, we die symbolically, succumbing to fear and
fortifying our conventional independence.

In the deeper strata of our being the subjective and
appreciative sides of care and attention have priority over
their objective and active sides. If each one of us is uniquely
durational and concrete, bearing forward a particular and
personal tradition, our specificity must be acknowledged by
others if their aid is to be adequate to our demands. Our
expressions must be attended to closely; others must attempt to take our viewpoint; and they must search for
tendencies within us that we have hidden from ourselves.
Only when they have come to appreciate us as who we
have become and have recognized the conflicts within us
can we trust them to help us express the possibilities of our
lives. Yet in everyday social life the general nearly always
takes precedence over the particular, the active over the
appreciative, the collective over the individual. Our physical incompletion triumphs over our concrete and polemical

being. We accord one another rights and duties, treat one another as functions, and adopt a defensive and calculating policy toward obtaining the goods we believe we require. The political structures that are imposed upon us and that we affirm while chafing under them are expressions of the motive of control, which arises from the fear that care and attention might be withdrawn if they are not motivated by an even greater fear of punishment. Many of us, of course, reach the point at which we believe that we will never be appreciated for what we have become; that, in fact, the appreciation of another person is not possible.

Deep within us, as Dostoevski glimpsed, is the dream of a utopia in which each one attends to, and cares for, the others, and in which the motive of control is no longer present in relations among persons. We long to relax our grip on ourselves, to abolish the conventional barriers that separate us from one another, to confess our crimes, and to proclaim our indigence openly. Yet fear, in its most hideous forms of mistrust and suspicion, keeps blocking us from taking the first steps toward realizing the vision. We flee to what Nietzsche called the "herd," the defensive alliance that unites us by symbols that stand over us, and by ritual humility toward suprahuman or infrahuman realities. We unite ourselves by references to a common source and destiny while ignoring the particular and contingent bonds that effectively link us together in relations of mutual dependency. We seek power and advantage, substituting compliance for care and servility for attention. Or we seek what is often called love, substituting emotional slavery and fear of rejection for appreciation of our uniqueness and concern for the expression of our individuality. The cry for care and attention is, perhaps, our first expression, the paradigm of our sociality. The others do not, cannot repond to it adequately.

Care and attention are the grounds of our continuity with others. That continuity is broken very early in our lives by betrayal. As infants our dependence upon others is stark and unrelieved by the conventions we later construct to conceal it and to provide us with a specious sense of independence. The infant is neither self-consciously trustful nor suspicious but has a kind of native and inherent trust that its call will be answered, that it will be given care and nurturance. Even after the infant has learned to speak and has become a child, capable of articulating demands and judging coherently, this trust, an offshoot of desire, may persist. The child may not yet be an individual, centered in a life of its own and defined by contrast to others, but may be aware of itself only as related to others. The others may not, perhaps, be entirely reliable, but they are present and ready to provide aid and comfort. But there will come a day when the others fail the child. They will not be there to answer the cry; they will harm the child; or they will impose something terrible on the child after all of its pleas and all of its resistance have been exhausted. At that moment the child will recognize for the first time its dependency and fragility, its status as a separate individual with its own life that must be ultimately taken care of, and attended to, by itself.

The individual is baptized by fear in the universal ritual of betrayal. From the moment that we have been betrayed by those upon whom our life depends we lose our original continuity with others, never again to recapture it innocently. We realize that we cannot trust anyone absolutely;

that there are sins we will never be able to forgive, though we may try; that we are essentially solitary; and that our own being is never of paramount importance for another human being. We enter then on a life that, for the most part, will be ruled by calculation and in which, if we are fortunate, we will struggle to overcome suspicion despite its stubborn permanence. Betrayal is the efficient or proximate cause of the conventional ego. It impels us to legislate for ourselves, in the first instance to lay down rules for avoiding future traumas, and later on to devise technical imperatives for taking advantage of others. We no longer live in the expanded present of desire but become aware of a self that must be protected against invasion and carried forward into a perilous future. We learn, slowly at first, to be mendacious, to keep much of our expression to ourselves, and most importantly, we repress desires and insights that would counteract our quest for security by making us unacceptable to others or too generous toward them. We become, in a word, autonomous, and life's native ideal of conscious completion is progressively replaced by the drive toward self-maintenance over time, expressed by the many variations of the motive of control.

In the aftermath of betrayal we enter into the human estate. We are as dependent as ever upon others for care and attention, but we no longer trust that they will help us willingly or appropriately. Sometimes we are suffused with innocent and exuberant affection, momentarily forgetting our fundamental solitude; but part of us is excluded from the rapture, vigilant for danger and poised to mobilize its arsenal of threat and ingratiation when warning signals appear. We become sensitive to the moods of our intimates, learning when to make demands, how to obtain what we desire, and when and how to defer our desires until more propitious moments appear. Long before we learn how to be instrumentally rational with regard to physical objects we have acquired impressive experience in how to get around others. Yet most often we are oppressed by our separation, at least in its earliest stages. We seek to restore our lost continuity with others, to believe that the betrayal was just an accident, and, most horribly of all, that the others just misunderstood us, that the grounds for trust would be restored if they only knew who we really were. We flee from the tragedy inherent in the betrayal by trying to make ourselves presentable to others and by showing them that we deserve their care. We become guilty about our suspicions and therefore become suspicious of ourselves. We desperately and pitifully grasp at straws, willing to believe the others when they tell us that they have our own best interest at heart, that they love us.

Our inner struggle for and against our individuality is almost always ignored by others, even when signs of it are readily observable in our contradictory claims and wildly vacillating moods. Those who are charged with our care are, at best, concerned with our physical health and psychological adaptation and, at worst, merely interested in bringing us under control and domesticating us. They do not question their right to "socialize" us, forgetting the terrible struggles they fought in order to stabilize their own individuality. Often oblivious of the fact that they have betrayed us, they blame us when we show insufficient gratitude for their sacrifices and teach us to lie to them. Biblical wisdom is, of course, correct. The sins of each generation are passed on to the next. We should forgive our elders, for they know not what they do. But children are not wise.

How can they forgive and be grateful when they have not yet even fully learned to be suspicious? The formation of our individual selves is a genuine tragedy. We deceive ourselves if we believe that there will ever be a time when children are not betrayed. Each life is absolute and insistent, demanding its own conscious completion, yet we depend upon others for that completion.

The ambiguities and ambivalences of our relations to others are compounded by the fact that we originally express ourselves only through them. Before we present ourselves in the world as distinctive persons defined by contrast with others we represent them by expressing their lives to ourselves and then projecting them into the symbolic past-present-future. Even the most severe betrayals cannot destroy the child's dependence upon others for the content of a conventional ego. The process of socialization is far more thorough than being conditioned to meet expectations or learning a language and certain moral and practical imperatives. Cognitive, moral, and affective capacities are developed within the matrix of a mutating self-concept, the substance of which is the personalities of others. We do not merely incorporate the desires of others into ourselves in response to rewards and punishments, but, as Freud noted, we identify with those upon whom we depend. Identification is the interior act in which we express another person to ourselves. It is prior to expression of ourselves as concretely individuated beings.

Adults encounter the growing child as an imperfect replica of themselves and then often strive to make that replica into what they themselves would like to be or would have liked to have been. The formation of the child's conventional ego is a political struggle waged by concerned adults and the child, both in alliance and against one another. The issue of this conflict is just who and what the child will represent and carry forward into future action. When social roles are not highly differentiated and there is little vertical or horizontal mobility, the battle to create the conventional ego will be muted and the significant adults will act as representatives of group authority. When significant adults are not concerned about the child, other agencies will intervene to mold the conventional ego, often haphazardly. The political struggle, which the term "socialization" characterizes only imperfectly, is most intense when adults compete with one another to define the child's personality and draw the meaning of their own existence from the child's future destiny. Such conflict, which has been a hallmark of middle-class child rearing in the West, subjects the child to agonies of choice, but just by virtue of those agonies, fosters heightened individuality. It is not possible for adults to efface themselves and attempt to encourage the child's native virtues and gifts. Although the child does indeed have a spontaneous interior dynamic and certain specific limitations and powers, its life is not sufficiently structured to express a conventional ego on its own. The child must be disciplined to know its limitations and told about its gifts. The responsibility of the adult is not to discourage identification or to take it for granted but to become a person who is worthy to be represented by the child.

The representative phase of our being means that before we take charge of our existence as separate individuals we have absorbed others into ourselves and have repeated many of their possibilities. We may extend Heidegger's insight that we are the null basis of our own existence to the observation that when we begin to choose for ourselves we decide within the confines of lives that are often alien to our own. What we do with our heritage may, if we overcome fear sufficiently, become our own responsibility, but we will never outgrow our tradition altogether. We are acutely aware of the differences between ourselves and others when we rebel against their plans for us or violate the commandments they have imposed upon us, but we are often oblivious of the extent to which our rebellions and crimes are supported in the examples of those against whom we do battle. Our first expressions of others to ourselves are so primordial that only the most rigorous self-criticism is capable of disclosing them. And even after our basic identifications have been revealed we often have no choice as to whether we will continue to represent them, so deeply rooted are they. At best we can affirm and modify them in accord with circumstances, on pain of dissolving ourselves into nothing.

Representation is a double-edged process, serving both as a means of self-control and as a way of widening our appreciation of life. We do not identify with others out of fear, at least primordially, and have begun to express them to ourselves before they have betrayed us. Betrayal, in fact, is so anguishing for us not only because we need completion in various respects, but because we have made those who betray us parts of ourselves, integral components of our growing concrete being. Had we not filled ourselves with the lives of others, we would feel no sense of betrayal but only pain. Had we no fundamental and implicit loyalty to others at the core of our being, we would not be so scarred by their infidelity toward us. In our ordinary lives, we often make the mistake of interpreting children as imperfect adults. The adult, however, must overcome suspicion in order to trust, whereas the child has no alternative but to trust. The child's trust, of course, is silent and unreflective. The act of identification is not an existential choice, made in the awareness of owning a finite life, but a spontaneous response to an inner impulse to express life's dynamic. The expression of other lives is turned over to the motive of control when, after betrayal, the child becomes circumspect toward others; but representation is originally innocent of fear and individuality.

Representation continues long after childhood, forming the greatest portion of our existence. Most of our decisions with regard to the course of our lives are not concerned with what we will do for ourselves but to whom we will deliver our existence. In economic relations, if we are fortunate enough to have choices at all, we decide whom we shall serve; in politics, we decide whom we shall support and allow to control us. Our bonds to others are far deeper in intimate relations, in which we deliver ourselves over to the sentiments, desires, interests, and opinions of others, often remaining unaware of how empty our lives would be if we were not perpetually serving them. We flee from acknowledging how much we effectively represent others, because we suspect that they are unreliable or that they might exploit or abandon us if they knew how much we depended on them for excuses to fill our days. Many of us, of course, desperately seek independence, so mistrustful have we become, by taking the high road of deliverance to symbolic meanings or the low road of egoism, whether aggressive or passive and mystical. God, cultural values, the good of the species, progress, historical destiny, universal goodness, and group survival and expansion are all diversions from acknowledgment of, and commitment to, the particular others upon whom we depend and for whom our supposedly disinterested activities are undertaken. Similarly, selfishness, however aggressive it may appear to be superficially, is a defensive strategy that involves systematic and purposeful ignorance of concrete dependencies. Behind the individualist lurks the wounded child who will "show them," the most selfish act of all being the child's dream of committing suicide and watching the others grieve, sorrow, and repent.

Life is relatedness, and for us the most significant and primal relations are with other human beings. Contrary to Sartre, hell is not other people, but their absence. Contrary to Heidegger, we are not thrown into the world, but borne out of it and inserted into a dense network of others. Contrary to Kierkegaard, we are not primarily relations of ourselves to ourselves, but at first relations of others to ourselves and later, though never completely, relations of ourselves to others. The great existentialists have contributed the most sensitive accounts of what we are when we are enslaved by the motive of control. They have swept away all of the symbols with which we provide ourselves with security, leaving us alone with a vacant ego consumed by fear and trembling, and a sickness unto death. By carrying individualism to its most critical extreme, they have shown that we have no justification for living but an act of resolute affirmation, revealing that control and the projection of ourselves into the future is not absolute, but an achievement. The existentialists have ignored, however, the fact that our solitude is the counterpoint to the theme of our interior union with others and that it arises only after we have been gripped by fear and exposed to betrayal.

Control is not the essence of our existence, but a modification of our fundamental expression of life that is generated by the mutual inadequacy of circumstances and others to ourselves, and of ourselves to circumstances and others. We attempt to remake others and circumstances to complete our lives, but first we create ourselves by restricting our lives conventionally. Self-control is the presupposition of practicality, which means only that we are fundamentally impractical beings.

Our existence is basically tragic because we carry within ourselves the memory of a time when we were not separated from others, when we were continuous with them, when we were not suspicious, and when we did not have to care for ourselves. In our everyday lives we suppress this memory and declare defiantly or bitterly our autonomy, or we project the memory into the future as an ideal. We take pride in our self-sufficiency or abjectly surrender ourselves to authority, all the while evading the challenge others present to us. They are unreliable, but so are we. They crave a lost union they can never recapture, and so do we. They struggle to keep themselves under control so that they can control us, and we do the same to them. Were we to attend to, and care for, one another, we might break the chains of our self-imposed enslavement. But though we are capable of generosity we can never forget betrayal and the terror of boundless fear.

## 4. MEANING

The root of control is time structured by meaning. In our everyday lives we are not often aware of the lived and expanded present in which we express a response to our involvement in the world; we exist beyond that present in a symbolic future limited by a goal. The time of ordinary practical life is the past-present-future, and of these three dimensions the future dominates the other two as the end to which they are the means. Submission to control implies that we have acknowledged the dangers inherent in our condition and that we have learned that we must attend to, and take care of, our own lives and decide what we will attempt to carry forward into action. As adults our incompletion tyrannizes both over our concrete being, silently and continually mutating out of the past, and over our polemical being, announcing our incessant struggle in each present to maintain control over ourselves against our own demands to overthrow convention and to express more of our lives. The practical viewpoint, defined by Bergson as the tapestry we weave between ourselves and our deeper being, consolidates us as actors, making us appear both to ourselves and to others as distinctive units, each one with a character and a predictable set of dispositions.

As the foregoing discussion was intended to show, we are not born as practical beings, but must be made and make ourselves independent actors. Infants do not project themselves into the past-present-future but exist in successive presents, depending upon others to maintain their temporal unities. They do not entertain meanings and seek to actualize them but express desires, are assailed by fears, experience pleasures, and suffer pains. Only after they experience betrayal do infants become children and begin to have what we think of as a human life, an existence ceaselessly directed toward the future. What we are pleased to honor as our autonomy is the cruel result of our separation from others and presupposes suspicion and mendacity. The origin of our ordinary three-dimensional time is the interior act of deferring a desire or placating fear by symbolizing a future situation. We conceal our act of laying up our treasures in the future from others and thus become opaque to them and, for the first time, lucid to ourselves. Our first efforts at practicality do not involve planning and calculation so much as waiting, hiding, and direct action against impositions, all of which are responses to fear. Later we learn to get our way by plotting strategies that circumvent threats.

The essence of practical life is the substitution of an imagined and symbolized future, a meaning, for the immediate and expressive response to concrete experience. From the practical viewpoint events do not call forth a unique response but are signs and indicators of dominations and powers. Practicality does not appreciate an experience for what it is to the fundamental self but attempts to integrate that experience into the structure of the conventional ego. The withering fear brought on by betrayal immobilizes life, shattering its innocence. A new synthesis, through which life can be carried on once again, emerges in the defensive construction of conventions. We are, as Aristotle observed, political animals, but only after we have been impelled to protect ourselves. The fear of violent death, upon which Hobbes based his argument for sovereignty, is merely a shadow or projection of the interior terror we feel when we have been abandoned to our own resources. We do not so much fear others as we are terrified of our own inadequacy and unreliability. The meanings we create to guide our conduct hold the terror at bay and provide us with confidence.

The primary condition of practicality is that we have

some meaning. Throughout the history of Western thought philosophers of life and conduct have sought to define the meaning that should or must guide our existence, deriving it from reason, experience, revelation, or some combination of them. Their efforts have, of course, been impressive, providing us with an extraordinary array of options for grounding our existence. For the most part, however, the philosophers of conduct have mistakenly defined us as essentially practical beings, neglecting the fact that practice presupposes conventions that are overlaid on life's insistent and unresolvable dynamic. Are we born to seek pleasure and avoid pain? All hedonistic and utilitarian doctrines break against the stubborn fact that each pleasure is finite, carrying the future pain of separation within it. Should we seek to rise above our inclinations and live for universal and rational duty? Rational ethics are dissolved by the stubborn particularity of each human being and merely offer an abstract structure in which we still must decide what to do in each specific case. Are we destined to contribute to a divine plan or historical purpose? If so, how do we account for that great portion of our lives which is antithetical or irrelevant to the grand design? Life lies behind and beyond any system that restricts it to a definite and exclusive meaning. Our native and inherent meaning is to complete our lives consciously, but this meaning can never be actualized because it is an artifact of our lost innocence. All of the meanings that we project ahead of us are partial and hence relative to life. Our fulfillment as living beings is in the past, while our fulfillment as syntheses of life and awareness is impossible or at least unintelligible to reason.

The method of traditional philosophies of life is what Bergson called analysis and recomposition. First our practical existence is divided into components, and then one or more of them is placed above the rest as a standard for conduct. For example, we may notice that we attempt to bring our circumstances under control through the use of tools so that we can gain a temporary physical completion. If we are impressed enough by this observation, we may attempt to derive all of our other activities from labor, making the sound point that if we did not organize to transform our environment to serve us we would not exist as a species from one generation to the next. Yet much of what we do has apparently little reference to labor and is equally necessary for our continued existence. For example, we do not seem to be able to get along without language, procedures for rearing children, and justifications for our existence. Out of each of our necessities as species beings can be made a meaning, supreme over all of the others and the core of an ideal to which we can commit ourselves. Whatever this exclusive meaning may be, it will be partial and will have to be supplemented, either implicitly or expressly, by others. Yet it will always serve the same function of controlling and restricting our possibilities so that we can act. When we analyze our lives and then recompose them according to a supreme concept, whether it is a definition of ourselves or an ideal, we forget that this concept is abstracted from life, which has a dynamic of its own, profoundly alien to practice and to what Bergson called the requirements of social life.

Most of our practical life is not conducted in reflective awareness of a supreme meaning to which our particular acts are related in a chain of means to the final end. For the most part, ultimate meanings are personal ideologies, providing us with comfort when we have failed, offering us independence from the demands of others, and mobilizing our energies to continue living when we skirt the boundaries of raw life or the abyss of pure attention. As Heidegger observed, we are usually sunk into everydayness, pursuing finite goals that connect with wider social projects of which we are not fully aware. It is a bias of intellectualism to believe that we are impelled to give an accounting of our lives to ourselves critically and in detail. We normally seek to have as much of our existence as possible taken care of autonomically by forming habits and depending upon others to take care of us through the performance of their expected functions. We know that we must eat and hence must obtain food. We know what is required of us to make the occurrence of certain disasters less probable and what others are likely to demand from us. But we do not usually ask ourselves why we continue to do what is necessary for us to eat, how the pleasures we seek fit into a more comprehensive meaning, and why we attempt to ward off certain disasters and meet certain demands while we blithely expose ourselves to other dangers and rebel against other claims. The conventional ego that we project into time is not often coherent and systematic but is, in contrast, a haphazard agglomeration of projects, most of which have been imposed upon us without conscious review and have resulted from threatening situations in the past.

Any expression of a desire or symbolization of the removal of a fear can be projected into the future and made into a meaning that controls conduct. The selection of which expressions will make up the content of any conventional ego is determined by a multitude of factors that are explored by such disciplines as sociology and psychiatry. We know that such devices as force, threat, bribery, and

flattery are useful, within limits, to control the content of
the conventional ego, and that despite the efficacy of these
devices early identifications are difficult to dislodge. We
also suspect that after we have summed up and coordinated
all of the circumstantial determinants of a person's meaning
there still remains a margin, which varies widely in its
extent, for arbitrary choice and revision. The conventional
ego is not a static entity but a tapestry that is continually
unraveling and being remade as the fundamental self responds to new events and memories reassert themselves
through dreams and fantasies, altering the designs that we
have woven for our lives. We have no absolute control over
the future, not only because our circumstances and others
can and will surprise us, but because we are fated to surprise ourselves.

No tendency in philosophy has revealed the conventional
character of meaning better than existentialism. The term
"existentialism" has been applied to a wide variety of writ-
ings, often advancing mutually incompatible interpretations, which are thematically united by a concern with the
individualized human being's encounter with life as a
whole. Taken in a broad sense existential themes can be
traced back to the thought of St. Augustine, who based his
system on the predicament of the individual confronting a
choice among faiths, and then in the modern age to Blaise
Pascal, who opposed the spirit of *finesse* (the demands of
the heart) to the spirit of logic (mathematical reason).
However, not until the nineteenth century did the problem
of the individual's meaning become a major concern of
Western thinkers in the works of Kierkegaard, Dostoevski,
Max Stirner, and Nietzsche, all of whom challenged pre-
vailing theories of historical destiny in the name of the

irreducible particularity of each individual. In the twentieth century existentialism became a broad philosophical movement, carried forward by such thinkers as Karl Jaspers, Heidegger, Marcel, Martin Buber, and Sartre, all of whom defended personal responsibility for decision against systems that purported to offer secure and stable meanings for action.

It is not possible to reduce existentialism to a set of doctrines, because it will always be possible to find a thinker who has been called an existentialist who disputes any specific thesis that might be put forward. What is important in the present discussion is to isolate and identify some themes expressed by many existentialists that are relevant to the nature and function of meaning in human life. Nearly all of the existentialists, whether they are theistic or atheistic, ontological or ethical, hold that the definitions and meanings through which human life is given purpose are created by human beings themselves in their successive practical choices. That we are beings who live by meanings, then, is, according to the existentialists, our essential characteristic; but they also hold that no particular meaning is necessary or rationally demonstrable. Existentialists reject the notion that knowledge is virtue, that we can identify our purpose through a cognitive discipline, that there are objective criteria for a good life in which all or even a few are capable of participation. Yet they insist, at the same time, that we need meanings or, in some cases, that we even require an ultimate meaning in order to exist.

The existentialist contribution to understanding our life has been to provide a description of the minimum structure of what Bergson called the practical viewpoint. For the existentialists we are fundamentally practical beings who are called upon to project ourselves into the future by attempting to actualize possibilities that we have chosen. Yet in deciding upon a meaning we are deprived of any cognitive security. There are no wise authorities who can tell us what we should do, and our own reason can provide us only with laws of efficient causation that exclude the category of purpose. Those who tell us that we have a specific destiny are no more profound than we are but are merely enslaved by their own will to subjective certainty and objective security. Existentialism, then, reveals the motive of control, the weaver of the tapestry of meanings deprived of any threads. We are left in the terrible situation of having to take charge of our own lives; having to care for, and attend to, ourselves; but with no hope of finding outside ourselves any justification for living. Only our own affirmation of life, seized from within, can, as Albert Camus noted, justify us.

The most significant implication of the existentialist description of our situation has to do with our temporal being. The projection of a meaning for which we live is the interior act by which we expel ourselves from the lived and expanded present of the fundamental self into the symbolic past-present-future of the conventional ego. For the existentialists, who abjure vitalistic intuition, there is no fundamental self but only a conventional ego, proceeding, in the most critical interpretations, from the nothingness of our origins to the nothingness of our death. Our time can no longer be structured by perspectives of transpersonal meaning, such as those provided by religious systems or secular philosophies of history, which insert us into a progression transcending our lifetimes and to which we can deliver ourselves. Instead, as Heidegger taught, we are awakened to the fact that we "temporalize time," that we are the creators of time because we are the creators of meaning. Our creation of meaning and time implies that we can, at any moment, resymbolize our purposes, that if we wish to live in truth we must be continually aware that we can revoke our commitments, unravel our present tapestry, and construct a new one. We are thrown back upon ourselves in each fleeting specious present, bidden to heal the split between subject and object or, in Sartre's terms, *pour soi* and *en soi,* in a new resolute action.

The critics of existentialism often oppose it on the grounds of its preoccupation with our bleaker moods and prospects, such as despair, anxiety, anguish, alienation, and death. Why, they ask, do the existentialists fail to balance their descriptions of our tragic side with our obvious successes and fulfillments? Such criticism is nearly always superficial and betrays the judgment that existentialists are unhappy people who have created a philosophy to justify their pessimism or, even more harshly, their personal inadequacies or inferiority feelings. The structure of the existentialist mentality, however, is the reverse of the way the critics interpret it. The existentialists have merely noted what happens to us when we criticize the meanings by which we have been living. When we find that we are, indeed, responsible for the content of what we project into the future, that our self-definitions are merely conventions, we become anxious about our future, we are anguished by our abandonment, we dwell in our finitude and essential solitude, we despair over a deliverance that we crave, and we choose under the shadow of our death. The fact that many human beings, including most philosophers, have not journeyed to the limits of the practical viewpoint and have not confronted the necessity of projecting a meaning that they know is self-created and conventional does not demonstrate that the practical viewpoint is supreme and unquestionable. Disputing the existentialists when one has not repeated their journey is equivalent to disputing the proofs of a mathematician when one has not attempted to reproduce them.

The grave limitation of existentialism is not that it grants some moods and conditions priority over others, but that it never breaks contact with the practical viewpoint and thus is enslaved by the motive of control. The existentialists have disturbed the security of everyday life by showing that we are not primordially objects to ourselves, but that we must make ourselves objects by projecting meanings. As Berdyaev noted, we become actors through a process of *objectification,* in which we first spontaneously and later deliberately annul what he called our "meonic freedom." The existentialists have shown that at the root of our efforts to control our circumstances and others is an act of self-control or, in their terms, an existential choice by which we affirm a particular and finite life through the selection of some possibilities rather than others. In sum, what they have argued is that prior to control is freedom or, to state the matter as Sartre did, that existence precedes essence. Yet because they were limited by the practical viewpoint, the existentialists did not place the perplexities and agonies of action in the context of life's wider dynamic, which reveals us as polemical, incomplete, and concrete beings. Rather than attempting to suspend the practical viewpoint as Bergson did and to attend to the processes that border, penetrate, and disrupt convention, they leave us in the situation in which the individual and separate self was born and to which we may, certainly, always be thrown back. The essential insight of existentialism is that we are abandoned to our own devices, that we have been betrayed by the world, but that we still must act. When interpreted from the viewpoint of life's dynamic, Heidegger's idea that we are "thrown" into the world and Ortega's notion that we are "shipwrecked" beings do not describe our primordial being but refer to who we are in the aftermath of betrayal. Bound to practice, the existentialists always look forward into the future, looking back to the past only when they succumb to the temptation to anchor themselves in a tradition—to repeat, as Heidegger often wished to do, a past possibility.

The existentialists are correct to dispute the presence of cognitive criteria for selecting meanings, to alert us to the choice between affirming and negating our lives, to insist that we acknowledge ourselves as the creators of symbolic time, and to thrust us back into the fear and trembling of our initial encounter with separation and individuality. They are mistaken, however, whenever they attempt to make the mere acknowledgment of our frustrated condition a virtue and the structure of that condition a guide for conduct. Concealed behind all of the concepts of "authentic existence" is the demand that we live in truth, that we take up the burdens of our existence despite their terrors. Although existentialists reject any positive definitions of our meaning, they commit the cognitive fallacy by enjoining us to live in the truth that any ultimate meaning is conventional. From the viewpoint of vitalistic intuition, however, practical life itself is never so supreme that it can prescribe any policy for us. Existentialism, then, does not offer a better way of life but merely the most critical description of who we are when we are consumed by the motive of control and have lost contact with the deeper and ongoing process of our life.

## 5. EXTERNAL CONTROL

Most analyses of control in human relations are concerned with how people control one another and their common environment rather than with how they control themselves. Yet the dynamics of self-control lie at the origins of the more external and readily observable methods and restrictions by which we maintain a transient and apparently objective order in our affairs. Action directed toward regulating others and circumstances presupposes the formation of a conventional ego, which is the repository of values, norms, plans, and strategies. How symbolization, which is required for us to be able to communicate meanings to one another, and, most importantly, to ourselves, was possible in a causal sense is a problem that should not concern philosophers. Scientists may attempt to discover the conditions antecedent to symbolization or the essential structure of symbolic systems; but their perspective will not allow them to absorb the meaningful into the meaningless, the final cause into the efficient cause, or the covert intention into the overt behavior. Myth provides more satisfying accounts of the origins of individuality and symbolic community, but it does not offer us critical and rational knowledge. Philosophers should be content with the datum that we propel ourselves into time and action by creating meanings and definitions to which we devote ourselves. The conditions that allow us to do this and the ultimate purpose, if any, of our practical life should be the concerns of science and myth, respectively.

Once we have solidified and instituted a conventional ego, we embark upon a life delivered over, for the most part, to actualizing a series of finite meanings. We insert ourselves into networks of social relations in which each of us is one among many actors submitted to disciplines of cooperation and domination, and vulnerable to a vast array of threats and sanctions. We are made aware immediately of the rewards we will receive if we comply with the demands of significant others and the punishments we will suffer if we are refractory. Even more important, we learn just what others consider rewards and punishments to be, and with our knowledge we become skilled in turning the weapons of our superiors against them. Insofar as we are delivered over to the motive of control, we are attentive to all the ways in which we can get around others, make them submit to us, placate them, and thus get our own way. Depending upon the meanings that compose the conventional ego, we will have to resort to mendacity, servility, force, and bribery to a greater or lesser extent. It is a problem for sociology and psychology to identify which particular methods we use to control others in different circumstances, which conventional meanings harmonize us with one another, and which ones make us mutually antagonistic.

To become functioning members of a group we must learn to calculate, to think hypothetically, to be politicians. The overt behaviors that social scientists observe and enumerate are merely the tip of an iceberg, most of which is buried in subjectivity. The greatest part of social control is accomplished in the silent anticipations and calculations of each actor considering the consequences of possible deeds and the dangers that may arise unbidden. Much of our inner life is consumed by prefiguring what others will do if we make a move. Will they ally themselves with us or seek to defeat us? How can we persuade or bully them so that they will make a sacrifice in our advantage? Beneath all of these optimistic calculations is the question, How can we keep them from abandoning or harming us? As much as we may pretend that our calculations are rational, the desperate mood in which we undertake many of them reveals that we are often neither certain of our own meanings nor sure of the meanings of others. The effectiveness of our control over others depends not only on our resources and technical skills but also on being sure of exactly what we want. Practical success depends upon a fine adjustment between certainty of meaning, knowhow, and propitious circumstances.

Politics provides the paradigm for practical life because what is ordinarily differentiated as political activity merely highlights the essential dynamics of social control. Political activity is concerned with the problematic, the unfinished, the disputed, the contingent. Political life involves the creation, maintenance, and destruction of conventions, as well as their enforcement, all of which are the same processes, on a grand scale, that absorb the self. Just as we often seek to stabilize the conventional ego by belief in the necessity or goodness of a particular meaning, so we attempt to bring one another under control by endowing the institutions that unite us with sacred or material sanction. We are frequently unaware of the political processes that lie behind everyday social life, because there is normally a complementarity between the contents of the conventional ego and regnant social conventions. Yet the ubiquity of police forces, churches, counselors, and lawyers should indicate to us how little of our social life is natural and spontaneous and how much of it depends upon repressive enforcement.

The motive of control is severely limited in most social relations by the contents of the meanings projected by social actors. If people have few conflicting desires, acknowledge one another's limitations, resign themselves to being exploited, and/or share the same ultimate meanings, they will reach a modus vivendi in which the fear of abandonment and exclusion will be muted and they will live in relative peace. However, beneath the tenuous social compact fear will lurk, ready to unleash the Hobbesian war of all against all whenever conventions are shattered or their enforcement is neglected. Social relations, as long as they are ruled by control, rest ultimately on mutual fear. The motive of control originates in the sense of betrayal and the birth of suspicion, both of which lead us to make others predictable servants of our individual demands to persist in time. As infants we are abused by others, and we fight back, first by separating ourselves from them, and later by exploiting them as means to the fullfillment of the ends we have projected. We engage in a power struggle that is no less intense if we find that our most effective strategy is submission to those who are stronger or to a common ideal. The implicit warfare of practical life is mitigated only by other primary motives, such as appreciation and sacrifice, which will be discussed in the following chapters. When we do not let these other motives temper control, we are possessed by Hobbes's ceaseless search for power after power.

A society based only on the motive of control would be

guided by suspicion and, therefore, by the struggle for advantage over others. Each would attempt to monopolize the means to act, not the fruits of action. Each would attempt to use the others as tools, knowing at the same time that the relation was reciprocal. Each would be an isolated individual, the owner of a monadic self, and the protector of all that could be incorporated into it. Perhaps such a society would not be marked by much violence, particularly if the strong combined to tyrannize the weak. But there would be no joy in the presence of others, no relaxation of defenses, no sympathy or compassion. The practical viewpoint is ruthless and isolating when it dominates life, bearing irremediably the curse of its origins. It is as ruthless when it sacrifices others and even the self in the service of an ultimate meaning or to the imperatives of an institution as when it seeks individual autonomy. Yet each one of us is a practical being, fated to be ruthless and to exploit others. We betray ourselves, however, when in reaction to the betrayals we have suffered, we understand ourselves resentfully as only practical beings. We should remember that only resentfully and regretfully do we enter upon practical life and that we are not exhausted by our actions.

# CHAPTER III

# APPRECIATION

From the moment at which we are consumed by fear and halt our flight into nothingness by erecting a conventional barrier between ourselves and others, and between our practical requirements and our deeper flow of life, we are delivered to the motive of control and begin to exist practically. Although much of our experience cannot be contained by our conventional fortress and bursts through it, we tend to suppress anomalies, either by turning our attention away from them or by reinterpreting them in accordance with the meanings we project ahead of us. Control is, indeed, tenuous, but we are often so skilled in repairing and reconstructing our battlements that we fail to question the supremacy of the motive of control itself, interpreting our inner conflicts as problems we should solve by reconceiving our goals or discovering or inventing more effective means to our ends. In our ordinary lives, we find that there is always more work to be done, always some task unfinished, always a new threat to the precarious equilibrium we have established. We never achieve a condition in which there are no excuses for taking responsibility for a situation or for preparing ourselves to take some future action. Our continuous and anxious anticipation of the future is based in our essential incompletion, the mysterious want that lurks at the core of our being; this anxious anticipation is the mood generated by the motive of control.

In everyday practical life we exist at the behest of what lies beyond us. Our senses are turned outward, and we are poised to react, most often mechanically, to the stimuli that appear unbidden. We interpret these stimuli in terms of the meanings we believe they have for us, perpetually sorting out the dominations from the powers, the corroborations from the anomalies, the fraudulent from the genuine. We dispose ourselves suspiciously toward our circumstances; we question our moments of apparent harmony, and we seek projects to keep us busy or we sink into torpor or sleep. At all costs we wish to avoid dwelling with ourselves and acknowledging and experiencing our polemical, incomplete, and concrete being.

The most rigid control to which we subject ourselves is the concern for achieving or maintaining a particular position in a network of social relations. Much of the time in which we are not involved in specific finite tasks is spent making ourselves fit to perform adequately before others. So fearful are we of losing our standing with others that we monitor our spontaneous judgments about them and ourselves, criticizing those that threaten our conventional stability and emphasizing those that fortify it. Even those who seek to live apart from others are often enslaved to convention, fearing so much their inability to control themselves that they feel safer in isolation. A silent shudder passes through us when we become aware of judgments others would disapprove, and we try not to think of them. We mock ourselves for violating our own conventions, often accusing ourselves inwardly of being weak or childish and preaching an interior sermon prescribing strength. The motive of control is often antithetical to what we believe to be the truth about ourselves, about others, and about our mutual relations. The conditions under which we receive care and attention, particularly of the most deprived sort, demand that we keep up conventions and conceal insights from ourselves. That form of sociality, which is created by the motive of control, is a defensive alliance grounded in fear. The price of being a member of such an alliance is submission to the rule of fear within oneself. We must convince others that we will not harm them or that we can call upon social authority to defeat them if they attempt to harm us. In either case we must put ourselves under sufficient control to make our reassurances, appeals, and threats credible.

We are constituted so that it is not possible for us to still life's insistent drive toward completion short of death. We are, however, capable of suspending our concern for social standing for periods sufficient to comprehend who we are when we are not enslaved to the conventional ego. As the creators of our symbolic selves, we also have the power to shift our attention away from them temporarily, if not to destroy them altogther. When we draw back from the conventional ego, we do not plunge into raw life, but we discover a different synthesis of life and awareness, one that is coordinated, not by the motive of control, but by appreciation.

## 1. APPRECIATION

In the history of Western thought there has been a continuous interplay between the active and contemplative orders of our existence. Plato's distinction between the philosopher and the king and his attempt to synthesize the two roles has been a persistent theme of Western philosophy, taken up in Aristotle's discussion of the virtues of the active and contemplative lives, and carried forward into the twentieth century by such thinkers as Husserl, who separated the natural attitude from the intuition of essences; by Bergson who divided the practical viewpoint from the intuition of concrete duration; by Heidegger, who opposed everyday involvement in finite tasks to resolute and authentic decision under the shadow of death; and by Santayana, who pitted the insistent primal will against detached spiritual freedom. In each of these cases the interpretation of the active life has been much the same, stressing the errors and deceptions that are integral to it and emphasizing its relativity and partiality. The great tradition has interpreted action as a sign of our imperfection, corruption, and vulnerability to accident and time. In contrast to the broad consensus about the active life, however, has been disunity about the mode of existence opposed to it.

For the Greeks, contemplative existence meant an ascension to the universal forms of reality, of which perceived appearances were merely imperfect exemplifications. The Greek spirit continues into the twentieth century whenever intellectual knowledge is opposed to action and this knowledge is interpreted as a guide to practice. Greek philosophy and its many contemporary derivatives are based on what was called in the preceding discussion the cognitive fallacy, the idea that the meaning of our existence can be defined conceptually and that conceptual knowledge offers valid prescriptions for a virtuous life. The ascensional dialectic of the Greeks begins within the everyday world of opinion and proceeds by pitting contradictory judgments against one another until a consistent and ideal hierarchy of knowledge is clarified. Both Plato's dialogical inquiry and Aristotle's aporetic method make of theory the alternative to practice, of true conventions the substitutes for deceptive and erroneous opinions.

The essential intention of Greek thought guides many other types of philosophy that dispute it on other grounds. For example, the Christian tradition of natural law, while it supplements natural reason with divine revelation, holds that knowledge of principles is supreme over practical judgments. Similarly naturalistic philosophies, which supplement reasoning with empirical observation, make of intelligence a guide to action, even when, as in the cases of Marxism and pragmatism, they assert the reciprocity of theory and practice. The root of Greek thought and its derivatives is that we are essentially practical beings for whom disinterested theoretical reflection is either a precious interlude from life's insistence or, most frequently in modern times, an essential moment in our struggle to master our circumstances. The great debate in Western thought between the rationalists who value the theoretical more than the practical life and the empircists who subordinate the intellect to the requirements of action is, in the terms of the present discussion, a family quarrel between partisans of the idea that knowledge is virtue. Whether contemplation is the good life or merely a necessary component of it, all of the followers of the Greek tradition make the basic assumption that intellection, rather than anything else, is the fundamental order of existence that is opposed to action.

The dominant Greek tendency has been opposed by very

few thinkers. In fact, one might argue plausibly that rejection of the idea that the fundamental division in our being is between theory and practice is enough to banish a thinker from the philosophical community. Philosophy itself, in many cases, seems to be exhausted in a desperate effort to hold the line against what it calls irrationalism. The term "irrationalism" has many meanings, the purest of which is the self-contradictory idea, itself derived from reasoning, that all intellectual knowledge is false. Some skeptics and mystics have, perhaps, asserted this principle on occasion, often merely to shock dogmatic rationalists into awareness of their own relativity. However, partisans of the Greek tradition have not confined themselves to pointing out the skeptic's self-contradiction; they have waged war against forms of thought that acknowledge the functions of reason but that challenge the ontological thesis that we are practical beings who are capable of resolving our conflicts by achieving an adequate cognition of our existence. The difference between dogmatic irrationalism and critical rationalism, which is usually glossed over by the dogmatic rationalist, is that the irrationalist disputes any claim for knowledge to guide practice, while the critical rationalist disputes only the claim that conceptual knowledge is capable of defining the meaning of our existence. Perhaps the united front of the Greek tradition is strengthened by confusing critical rationalism with dogmatic irrationalism, but such obvious polemical benefits are at the expense of understanding.

In the twentieth century the major challenge to the Greek spirit has not been skepticism, which itself is one of the possibilites of opposing theory to practice, but vitalism. When Bergson questioned the practical viewpoint, he did not do so in terms of intellectual contemplation but by virtue of an intuition that revealed to him the dynamics of a life that was indifferent and even antithetical to the requirements of action. Bergson accepted the empiricist's claim that theory is an instrument of practice but rejected the notion that we are fundamentally practical beings. He discovered behind the tapestry of rules, norms, and self-definitions the "fundamental self," which is a continuously mutating synthesis of heterogeneous qualities explicable neither in terms of mechanical causation nor in terms of teleological design. The fundamental self, then, could not be defined conceptually but could only be experienced. Bergson's great discovery was that we are not primordially practical beings who are capable of transcending active life in order to contemplate its structure and laws; rather, we are impractical and appreciative beings whose first encounter with the world is sympathetic and immediate. Our intellect, for Bergson, is merely an extension of our active and purposive life, performing the function of clarifying the circumstances in which we are embedded so that we can transform them to our advantage. The fundamental self, our deeper being, is, however, unconcerned with advantage, but merely changes spontaneously in response to its own interior dynamic. Bergson of course believed that we are, for the most part, fated to be absorbed in practical life, and he honored the intellect as the most useful aid to our collective survival. Yet he did not believe that the intellect could provide us with an ultimate meaning, all conceptual meanings being figments of the conventional ego.

Bergson also recognized, as did Kant, that the intellect is equivocal, that it is a double-edged sword that can always strike back at us and destroy social life. In his *The Two Sources of Morality and Religion* he argues that for human beings the intellect performs that same function of securing species survival that instinct performs for other animals. However, he observes that while instinct conspires to make animals behave in accordance with the collective good, the intellect individualizes each human being and sets each one against the others. We are capable of cooperation, but we are also delivered over to conflict. Our common life, then, is a continuous process of rebellion and reconciliation, marked by compromises and defensive alliances, in which each individual is subordinated to symbols and mythic meanings, only to overthrow them when they frustrate a powerful expression. The intellect is not, for Bergson, a faculty by which we liberate ourselves from life and comprehend its meaning but an imperfect organ of a precarious being. We can trust the intellect no more than we can rely upon our successive and often contradictory desires to carry us successfully from one present into the next. Thus, contemplative knowledge is not a sure guide to virtuous conduct, because reason looks equally toward the requirements of social life and the individual's separate advantage. Convention and myth bind us together far more than rational knowledge, which is adequate only for understanding and manipulating physical reality.

Bergson thought that beneath the superficial and defensive unity of our everyday practical lives there was a more basic continuity between ourselves and others that was rooted in the fact that we all participate in life. He interpreted life as an absolute reality, a vital impetus, which individuated itself into a variety of species and organisms. We need not affirm Bergson's metaphysics to recreate his intuition and to acknowledge that we are linked to one another not only by exchange, power, deference, and obligation but also by a native sympathy. Bergson's great mistake was to claim that life is self-sufficient, that it is the only reality. Thus, he was never able to account for the emergence of self-consciousness and the conventional ego. He attempted to explain individual consciousness by the resistance of matter but could not fill in the steps between frustration and practical control. The present discussion, while it owes much to Bergson's work, rejects the idea that life is self-sufficient and argues instead that we are syntheses of two heterogeneous realities: life and awareness. Here the fundamental self is not raw life but the expression of life's dynamism, and the conventional ego is the control of that expression generated by fear. Both expression and control demand that we be aware of life, that we be able to resist the incessant and mutating flow of life long enough to create an expanded present, a span of attention, in which we can participate in an experience as a meaningful durational unit. Bergson's intuition, then, is merely a shift of attention by which we turn away from the control of life and toward its own dynamic to appreciate it and to express its structure to ourselves.

At the outset appreciation is best considered negatively as a relaxation of control, not as a motive separate from control that challenges and conflicts with it. The appreciative mood is marked by a suspension of concern for the future and even more fundamentally by a suspension of concern for making oneself adequate to project oneself into the future. Appreciation demands that we desist from judging ourselves by conventional standards, whether they are derived from the expectations of others or from our own attempts to keep ourselves under control by creating partial meanings. When we appreciate, then, we cannot be absorbed in a task that demands our concentration and narrows our attention to a particular sequence of means and ends. Even more important, we cannot be engaged in planning a future act, calculating the costs and benefits, and comparing ourselves with an ideal standard of importance. We must have temporarily stilled fear and have relaxed sufficiently to mute our autonomic reactions to external stimuli.

Appreciation suspends the mood of anxious anticipation that rules our everyday practical life, substituting for it a quiet receptivity to the contents of experience and the spontaneous judgments we express about those contents. Only when we are relieved of anxious anticipation do we understand how pervasive this mood is. Ordinarily we are delivered over to the symbolic past-present-future, disguising our fear of abandonment by prospective linkages to others and circumstances. We can never be certain that our relations to the world are durable, and thus we must continually attend to those relations and care for them, primarily by creating a conventional ego that meets the requirements of others and that will protect us from involvement in dangerous situations. We are so afraid of succumbing to our basic fear of being left alone by ourselves without relations that we disperse our concerns into partial fears, each of which is relative to a particular bond to the world. However, as much as our care may be fragmented into responses to specific threats, the entirety of our practical life is suffused by anxious anticipation, a free-floating mood always in search of an object to which to attach itself and ever vigilant for signs that conventional unity is about to unravel.

The domination over our practical life of the motive of control and its accompanying mood of anxious anticipation accounts for why Bergson thought it so difficult to abandon, even momentarily, the practical viewpoint and to attend to life itself rather than to the possible objects of activity. Bergson believed that intuition is an extraordinary event, not a procedure that can be taught as a method. It is perhaps the case that intuition is not democratic, that many, if not most, people are too consumed by fear to relax the grip of control over their lives. If so, then appreciation is a gift we received unintentionally from those who cared for us when we were infants and who did not terrorize us so much that we lost contact with ourselves.

When anxious anticipation is replaced by receptivity to the present, we are free to appreciate our life for what it is, not for what we wish it to be in our conventional definitions. The appreciative mode of being is difficult to describe conceptually because it involves the effort to grasp the structure of our life as a whole at the same time that we are participants in it and, at least in part, creators of it. The motive of appreciation is only imperfectly understood when such terms as "disinterest," "detachment," and "contemplation" are applied to it. Certainly, appreciation is disinterested, detached, and contemplative in the sense that it renounces calculation, planning, anticipation, and advantage, but it is not directed toward the dispassionate observation of an object or event. Far from being dispassionate, appreciation is intensely passionate and, more important, compassionate, emphasizing the felt union of subject and object, subject and other, subject and self. To appreciate life's interior dynamic we must involve ourselves in it while we attend to our expressions of it. Appreciation requires liberation from our fear of knowing what life is, not from our particular desires, our pleasures and pains, and our particular relations to others, all of which compose the content of the life to which we attend.

Appreciation is a way of knowing that reverses the tendency toward theoretical contemplation. Conceptual thinking is a variation of the motive of control, in which we abstract from the particular object or event characteristics that will allow us to classify it with others and to predict its future relation to us. We hope, by our theoretical activity, to bring order to the blooming and buzzing confusion of experience, to make it intelligible, and finally to make it malleable and tractable and thus put it under control. Appreciation does not abstract from life but attends to our spontaneous expressions and judgments of it, both as a whole, through prophetic vision, and in the details of its incessant polemical conflict, drive toward completion, and concrete particularity. Appreciation, then, is the mode of being in which the structure of our being is revealed to us. No more than control is it a form of pure thinking; it is, rather, inextricably bound to the specific mood of receptivity and relaxation, just as control is permeated by the tension of anxious anticipation. The kind of knowledge toward which appreciation aims is indicated by such terms as "sincerity" and "honesty." However, sincerity and honesty refer here, not to the absence of conscious mendacity, but to the expression of judgments freed from the constraints of practicality. Appreciation aims at telling us who we are, not at informing us about what we must, might, or should do.

Appreciation, although it aims at self-knowledge, is not a retreat into the precincts of the private self. The kind of self-inquisition that is often called introspection, in which we review our failures and successes, compare ourselves with competitors or models, and torture ourselves with judgments that make us ashamed or guilty is always centered in the conventional ego and does not provide us with insight into who we are but merely with practical incentives to secure our standing among others in network of social relations. Similarly, when we withdraw to the safety of our own interior dialogue and draw up bills of particulars against those whom we believe have wronged us, or when we reassure ourselves that we have done what is necessary to secure care and attention from others, we are subservient to the motive of control and witnesses to its ceaseless work of constructing, maintaining, and altering an interior regime. All of the activities in which we judge ourselves according to norms are variations on the theme of what Rousseau called *amour propre,* the attitude in which we derive our worth from our social standing. Introspection never penetrates to the level of consciousness at which we recover our *amour de soi,* the native confidence that we are irreplaceable, unique, and concrete beings whose intrinsic value does not depend upon deeds.

The privacy of introspection, even when it passes beyond contingent and relative social relations to an encounter with our finitude and our anguish over the absence of an ultimate meaning, reveals nothing but the agony of practical life. As long as we are projecting ourselves forward and backward in symbolic time we are not ourselves, our own, but merely one-among-many individuals. Heidegger, who mounted the most devastating and thoroughgoing critique of everyday life, did not penetrate beneath convention to appreciation. In *Being and Time* he argued that when our being-toward-death is disclosed to us we are thrown back into a situation in which we can no longer rely upon the maxims of others to determine our destiny but must take responsibility for existence by ourselves through resolute choice. Yet he admitted that such resolute choice would have to be in terms of the ongoing historical projects of everyday life. For Heidegger, then, authentic existence is just a modification of "everydayness." We individualize ourselves before our own death only so that we can reenter the present network of social relations responsibly. We find nothing in our journey back to ourselves but the truth that we are the "null basis of our own existence," that we are radically dependent upon the conventional or "they" self for the meaning of our individual being. In Heidegger's vision, at least as he described it in *Being and Time,* we are destined to, and exhausted by, the conventional society of fictions and functions.

Heidegger's vision of our existence is so crucial because it distills the essence of modern philosophy, which has, from its beginnings in the thought of Hobbes and Descartes, delivered us over unremittingly to the practical viewpoint. Heidegger carries out a thorough and uncompromising mundanization of philosophy, sweeping away conceptions of the infinite, ideals of perfection, and notions of salvation, leaving us alone with ourselves but fated to live among others. His rich descriptions of the anxiety that attends our solitude and the guilt we experience when we realize that we are inadequate to the demands of the world and cannot hope to be compensated for our sufferings (that we are not justified) offer the most acute insights available to us into the sense of betrayal that impels us to enter upon a life ruled by control. But although these descriptions take us to the limits of practicality, they are based on introspection, not on intuition, and merely record the observations of someone who was sensitive to convention but could not, even momentarily, liberate himself from its tyrannical grip. Heidegger was, at least, honest about practical life, rejecting the philosopher's temptation to be a priest and to invent a myth of salvation that would conceal our essential incompletion. Instead he offered us the thankless task of taking responsibility for our existence without any expectation of reward and with the certainty that we are fundamentally no-thing.

If appreciation is not introspection, neither is it the revelation or disclosure of the unconscious under the methods of depth psychology, although when life is guided by the appreciative motive one of its possibilities is to uncover past desires, fears, relations, and events that have been repressed. Psychiatry's aim is therapeutic, and its inquests are guided by the principle that self-defeating behavior in the present can be explained and perhaps eliminated by discovering its roots in past relations. Each psychiatric theory identifies a specific set of relations that are supposed to account for the problems people cannot resolve on their own and defines a norm by which the health of a personality can be evaluated. Alfred Adler's idea that we tend to overcompensate for our inferiority feelings, Freud's notion that we fight a political struggle for affection within the family, and R. D. Laing's theory that we struggle to protect ourselves from the contradictory demands of those upon whom we depend are all examples of attempts to show why we often cannot act effectively and consistently to actualize finite aims. Such explanations, when we apply them to our own lives, are not the results of appreciation but merely efforts to remake the conventional ego so that it will be better constituted to secure our standing in social life. This does not mean that psychiatry is false but only that its explanations remain on the level of practical life and as such must be judged pragmatically on the basis of how well they fit us to act among others. The great psychiatrists had profound insights into our fragility and the tenuous character of the conventional ego. Which of us has not been assailed by inferiority feelings? Which of us has not overcompensated by asserting, at least on occasion, that we are invincible when we are really pitifully vulnerable? Which of us does not cherish the secret hope that we might cease deceiving ourselves and others and admit at last that our symbolic reassurances are merely brittle masks? Each of the great psychiatric theories is true for each one of us, though not simultaneously, because we all have been violated and diminished in many different ways, and we all have sought to defend ourselves from fear by repressing our frustrated desires.

Appreciation converges with psychiatry when we relax control over ourselves sufficiently to remember how we were violated in the past and how we constructed specific defenses to conceal from ourselves our fear of abandonment. Psychiatry's major contribution has been the discovery that the conventional ego is not completely or even primarily an instrumentally rational response to our incompletion but that it is also a mendacious fabrication we construct to ward off fear by concealing our past from ourselves. When we are delivered over to the motive of control, it is not possible for us to remember the past we have repressed; only when we become receptive to our life do we recover the particular conditions under which we became practical and later maintained and fortified the conventional ego. However, while psychiatric remembrance is a possibility for appreciation, it does not exhaust the appreciative motive. The disclosure of repressed traumas and desires and the identification of defense mechanisms is the way we appreciate the past, but appreciation may also focus upon the present and the future.

Perhaps the closest approximation to appreciation in the history of Western philosophy is Spinoza's view of our lives from the standpoint of eternity. According to Spinoza, our life is ordinarily ruled by desire and our knowledge is relative to our quest to achieve pleasure and avoid pain. Yet we are capable also of stilling life's insistent drive temporarily and of contemplating our existence as a whole. For Spinoza the view from eternity does not involve the intuition of essences or the participation in ideal forms; it is a reflection on life itself that shows its limitations and partiality and that makes it relative to an indifferent and perfect infinite substance. Spinoza's vision is different from appreciation because it transcends passion and is motivated by the cool and contemplative intellectual love of God. Yet were we to contemplate our life without the support of an idea of perfection and a notion of an infinite substance, we could no longer be dispassionate but would instead become compassionate toward ourselves and others. We would not experience an intellectual love of God but a vital love of ourselves and others, not only in spite of, but because of, our imperfection and the conventional character of our practical selves. We would then begin to appreciate.

The motive of appreciation is to know ourselves as who we are after we have banished from our consciousness all of the constructions that have been erected by the motive of control and that separate us from ourselves and others. Through recovering the past that we have repressed appreciation discloses our concrete being, the unique autobiography of each one. Through quietly struggling against anxious anticipation and opening up receptivity to our spontaneous expressions of life, appreciation reveals our polemical being, in which the fundamental self contends with the conventional ego in a battle between sincerity and mendacity. Finally, by the withdrawal of attention from subservience to future goals and our standing in social relations, appreciation acknowledges our essential incompletion and offers us a glimpse of the basic tragedy of our life. The appreciative motive in its purity renounces the support of any idea that provides security, even the idea of an alien God whose perfection we can never experience although we can make it an object of intellection. Introspection takes us away from everyday tasks only so that we can perform them more resolutely. Depth psychiatry relaxes us only so that we will be better fit to act consistently. Intellectual love transcends our partial concerns only so that we can be reconciled to our finitude. All of them are bound to the practical viewpoint by their intent to discover knowledge that might make us virtuous. Appreciation seeks only to observe and sympathize, not to transform.

## 2. THE STRUGGLE TO APPRECIATE

Receptivity to life is not won without an intense interior struggle against the motive of control. We are continually making judgments about our life, both with regard to its particular vacillations and with regard to its totality, which are at variance with the rules we have legislated to keep our conduct within consistent and socially acceptable limits. These judgments are not necessarily or even mostly unconscious in the sense that they are mute and elude awareness. When we are eating a tasty meal, for example, we are aware of the content of the pleasure we experience, but rarely do we involve ourselves so completely in the act that we attend to its entire context, our multiple sensory responses, and the rhythm of tension and release. We enjoy only a small portion of the meal, perhaps a simple and single dominant taste or texture; we barely experience the visual beauty of the food, its aroma, and the internal changes we undergo as we become full. The act of eating, for us, is not usually an end in itself that opens up an expanded present but is an event within a daily schedule or round, preceded by some events and succeeded by others. As we eat we are often urgently recalling something that happened in the recent past and seeking to divine its meaning, brooding over the frustration we met, or congratulating ourselves on our success. Or we may be preparing for what we must do next. Even if we have stilled our concern for the past and future, we remain alert for threatening stimuli and ready to mobilize our defenses and center ourselves in the conventional ego. The diversion of our attention from the expanded, continuous, and lived present toward the symbolic past-present-future when we eat applies to all of our other activities in everyday life. Most of the content of the lived present is lost to us, even though we may glimpse fragments of the qualitative unity.

The same factors that inhibit us from appreciating a pleasurable activity block even more our appreciation of another person. When we converse with someone, we are often so concerned to convince them that our interpretation of an event is correct or, more fundamentally, that we deserve to be acknowledged, that we attend to our own performance and neglect their struggles to express themselves, lose sight of the loose ends and incomplete meanings in their discourse, and deaden our sensitivity to their tacit intentions. We take their statements at face value and do not separate their spontaneous expressions from their efforts to be conventionally acceptable. We organize the conversation around a topic common to both of us, at best gleaning our various contributions to compose a discussion and at worst allowing our statements to be divided into separate and discrete monologues. We are frequently constrained by memories of past slights and insults and by projections of our future relationship, and so we divert much of our attention to censoring our responses in accordance with our calculations. Even if we are disposed to appreciate the other we must continually monitor our expressions to make sure that the other does not become suspicious of us and resort to defensive strategies. We must provide reassurances, make apologies, and offer justifications opportunely so that the encounter will not break off because either party has been rebuffed. We must attempt to maintain the standing both of ourselves and of the others in the relation, especially if we wish it to continue for more than one encounter. The relation, then, and our expectations for it take on a being independent of our concrete and present expressions, just as a diet transcends our enjoyment of any particular meal. In everyday life, ruled by the motive of control, the concrete presence is absorbed by the symbolic projection, the lived present by the past-present-future.

Control is necessary if we are to project ourselves from one present to the next. We must be ruthless, selective, and exclusive in order to act, and we must act in order to live. Thus, relaxing control is fraught with danger. Not only are we assailed by various partial fears, to which we respond with an arsenal of defenses, but we are also consumed by a deeper and usually hidden fear that we will not be able to rise to the occasion, that we can throw ourselves or be thrown into a state of consciousness in which we will not be able to be practical. We look back to the moment of betrayal when we were helpless and desperately fight against the tendency within us that would draw us into the lived present and abandon us to our sincere expression of it in all of its richness and complexity. If we enjoy our meal too much, we fear that our desire for food will vanquish our will to lose weight. If we reveal ourselves to others or, even more important, reveal them to themselves or tempt ourselves to appreciate who they are, we fear that we will lose our friends. If we are too receptive to the present event and our spontaneous response to it, we fear that we will lose our hard-won conventional self and with it our future.

We have no initial difficulty in becoming receptive to the lived present because the dynamic of our life is continually drawing us into it through the naive search for completion. Yet once we have experienced fear and betrayal we begin to block automatically all of our tendencies to abandon ourselves to the event. Our essential incompletion means that we cannot be fulfilled by any particular relation to the world but require symbolic substitutes for an absent plenitude. Appreciation is dangerous because it repudiates the symbols that provide us with security, leaving us only with the current experience and the knowledge of its finitude and our fragility. We struggle to keep ourselves under control, to keep our distance from the blundering optimism of life and the tragic wisdom that attention to our incompletion evokes.

If we succeed in loosening our grip on ourselves and withdrawing attention from the past-present-future, we are not pulled back into peaceful contemplation of natural or divine harmonies but into life with all of its contradictions and complexities. Perhaps the most intense appreciation we can have is that of our terror before our fundamental solitude. There are times at which we are in the company of others, conversing idly with them, maintaining one another's standing in the network of relations, and bored with, or indifferent to, the discussion. As we sit and observe the others with a certain languid detachment we may notice how much of their discourse is conventional, how much they are presenting themselves to us to gain our approval, or, even worse, how much they are presenting themselves only to themselves in an effort to confirm a conventional ego. We become aware that they are imprisoned in a closed and vicious circle of suppressed resentment or in desperate efforts to compensate for inferiority feelings or in unconscious strategies to bend others to their wills through servile ingratiation or subtle threats. We begin to wonder whether we have ever known them at all and whether they have ever had any insight into who we are, whether we have ever cared for them or they for us, except conventionally and practically.

Suddenly the others seem unreal to us. They appear to be apprentice actors going through routines mechanically or even to be mechanical toys who wind themselves up repeatedly and then perform programmed motions and emit programmed sounds. Then we begin to become possessed by a fear more deeply rooted than any of our everyday anxieties. What if one of them addresses a comment to us? How will we answer them? They are impenetrable. We cannot reveal to them how we have expressed them to ourselves. We cannot be honest and tell them how much of their lives is suffused by resentment or inferiority feelings. We cannot tell them how dominated by convention they are and how much we pity them. We are not capable of arguing, yet we also cannot summon the practical control to become a part of their stratagems or to play our own habitual games. We have suspended the motive of control and appreciate the present situation for what it is, but the others are still enslaved to control and would interpret any sincere response of ours to the situation as an attack upon their dignity or as a sign of mental illness. We are isolated by our dangerous knowledge that we hunger to communicate but cannot. If we do not leave the situation we may experience a horrible and infinite distance from the others. Physically they may even be touching us, but socially they are separated from us by a gulf that we cannot span through any action.

As we become aware of the abyss over which we can throw no rope, our attention turns from the others to ourselves. The situation recedes from us; the others are no longer vital presences to us but hollow voices and abstract shapes. They are no longer real, because what is real for us is that to which we can forge relations. Having lost our relations to the others temporarily, we drift back into ourselves and toward nothingness. It is then that we experience the terror, not of our future death, but of the isolation of our attention. For a moment our attention is severed from our life, and it is sucked back into the mysterious void from which it emerged. Our life fights back desperately, seeking to anchor us once again in the world and to reestablish the conventional ego. We experience a desolating nausea, not Sartre's nausea at the messy and flawed and arbitrary jungle of existence, but the vertigo of losing our hold on life. Life was too much for Sartre, the extreme practical individual, but it is too small and mean and petty for appreciation. We struggle to stave off the nausea and to focus our attention on some finite task. We force ourselves to get up and stretch or to yawn or to pour ourselves a drink or smoke a cigarette, and we return to the practical viewpoint. Meanwhile the discussion has continued around us aimlessly and pointlessly. Our agony has been silent and invisible. Nobody knows that we have died and have been reborn, that we have appreciated the fragility or life and the nothingness of attention. We reenter the conversation, at first tentatively and then more securely until we no longer distinguish between the conventional and the fundamental.

Under other conditions the appreciative release of control is far more limited, stopping short of the dissolution of our relations to the world and merely plunging us into the lived present. The present may embody any of the indefinite number of experiences that are possible for us. An experience here means a durational unit that binds together in an inextricable synthesis an event and our response to it.

Only when we project ourselves into the symbolic past-present-future do we separate a cognizing, calculating, and analyzing subject from a cognized object abstracted from its concrete relations and then placed in various sets of ideal relations. By expressing our responses to events spontaneously we incorporate them into ourselves, fusing them with the past that we carry into the present rather than separating them from our lives as independent entities that are parts of an objective world described in terms of claims of efficient causation or means to external ends. Our possibilities for expression range from the contemplation of beauty to the revulsion against imperfection and decay. When we observe what from the practical viewpoint would be the same scene, our attention may be focused upon its density, contingency, aimlessness, and arbitrariness, or upon its immanent structure and completion. We may be consumed by Sartrian nausea and learn the lesson that only our efforts bring order to the confused jungle of existence, or we may be awed by what Kant called the "purposeless purposiveness" of natural rhythms and configurations. Appreciation offers us no consistent description of the structure of the world but only knowledge of all of the different relations of our life to it. Each present embodies its own expression of quality, its own judgment of the relation of life to the world. The judgments may be mutually contradictory, but the appreciative motive does not seek to reconcile them into hierarchies of reality and appearance or of knowledge and opinion. Each one stands as an absolute expression of life, depending upon the conjunction of its unique past and its involvement in the present event.

The motive of appreciation is inclusive and receptive, in principle, to every one of our expressive responses to the world except the withering fear of solitude and abandonment that submits us to the motive of control. Yet each particular appreciation of our life is absolute and sufficient unto itself, constituting a spontaneous judgment on the lived present. The two essential features of appreciation—its inclusivity in general and its specificity in particular—work against control, which is exclusive with regard to our possibilities and tentative, doubtful, and insecure about our interpretation of each passing event. Control allows us neither to welcome judgments in conflict with the conventional ego into our practical life nor to abandon ourselves to the pursuit of a desire or the discharge of an impulse without care for the consequences for our standing in social relations and our symbolic goals. The root of our polemical being is the struggle between appreciation and control, desire and fear. The struggle to appreciate, then, is the battle to overcome fear of our own expressions and judgments about life.

## 3. TRAGEDY

One of the possibilities for appreciation is prophetic vision of life's inner dynamic and destiny. When we relax the hold of control upon our lives, our attention may be directed, not to our participation in a particular event or to the tyranny of convention over us, but to the structure of our life itself. From the practical viewpoint dominated by control we are projected ahead of ourselves toward a future that we symbolize as a meaning. Appreciation, which suspends the conventional ego, challenges the reign of meaning, substituting for it insight into our essential tragedy. Tragic vision involves awareness of our irremediable incompletion, of our dependence upon our relations to the world and to others, and of our native ideal of an impossible conscious fulfillment in which all of our desires are satisfied, all of what we can appreciate is carried forward into action, and yet we continue to live.

Only when we allow the appreciative motive to guide us do we sound the depths of our existence and express our sincere judgment about our lives. The insight that all of our meanings are conventional, that, in Camus's terms, there is no response to our demand for unity, can be achieved without ever leaving the practical viewpoint, but we cannot grasp its significance until we suspend the motive of control. Appreciation puts us on the other side of practice, not beyond it in an ideal harmony, but behind it through a surrender of projection. The prophetic vision of appreciation is of the fundamental absurdity of the practical viewpoint, of the inadequacy of any symbolic meaning to fulfill our lives, and of the inadequacy of life to its native ideal. When we appreciate our condition, we find that we are fated to be incomplete and that all of our attempts to become self-sufficient or to become a necessary part of a wider self-sufficient totality are vain. We understand that if indeed we are part of a plan or design that transcends our lives, we cannot symbolize its meaning and cannot know whether it is alien to our hopes or consonant with them. We encounter the mystery of our existence and learn that we can devise no convincing explanation of why attention has found a dwelling in our life, why we are fated to desire what contradicts our being, and why we must be subject to fear and its consequence, the rule of good and evil. We grasp the essential tragedy that we are fundamentally impractical beings who are destined to a practical existence in which we must mendaciously convince ourselves that our persistence or the persistence of a group to which we belong or of some work that we have achieved is important. We feel simultaneously our attachment to the world and to others and the ultimate frustration of our hope to continue it.

The mood in which we appreciate the incompletion and tragedy of life distinguishes the appreciative motive from both religious faith and existential rebellion. Appreciation of our limitation and ultimate frustration is neither despairing nor resentful but sad and compassionate. The religious existentialist is as acutely aware as the vitalist of our contingency, dependency, and fragility, and of the vanity of our attempts to save ourselves through our own activities to actualize meanings, but responds to these insights by a leap of faith in a God, who despite all appearances and reasonings upon them is concerned about our plight and cares for us. Without faith the religious existentialist is thrown into despair and is, perhaps, tempted by suicide. Such a person cannot live with the insight that our efforts might have no final meaning, that each one of us might not live for some purpose, and that our synthesis of life and awareness might irrevocably perish. Thus, the religious existentialist, having anguished over our own inadequacy to ourselves, places trust in a supreme actor, whose practice is perfect, who is consciously complete. The existential rebel also suffers despair but responds to it by passionate embracement of our absurd condition in an act of self-affirmation and defiance from which resentment against our abandonment is never wholly absent. Both the religious existentialist and the existential rebel interpret us as practical beings who must be saved from despair and somehow be provided with incentives to continue acting despite the absence of rational guarantees of fulfillment. Both are enslaved by the Greek tradition, even as they react against the principle that we can know our meaning rationally. For our basic fear before our solitude and the nothingness of attention they substitute the deprived category of despair, which is merely the cognitive judgment that we have no grounds for hope in the fulfillment of our deepest yearnings.

The appreciative insight into the absurdity of our life is not achieved in the anxious quest to regain a foothold in practical existence after the conventional justifications for action have been revealed to be arbitrary and conventional. When we appreciate life's dynamic and its tragedy, we are not involved in the effort to control ourselves, to make a resolute choice, and to determine ourselves as individuals, but we are removed from life's insistent drive and able to sympathize with it. We are no longer concerned with our particular destinies and with our responsibility to choose whether we believe or despair, live or die. Rather, our individuality is no longer important to us, and we glimpse ourselves as individuations of life who are no different from any other individuations in our essential structure. As we grasp our dependency, contingency, and limitation we are infused with sadness and compassion, not despair or resentment. We observe our self-importance and understand it as a response to fear and betrayal. We pity ourselves, not by virtue of a comparison between our failure and some possible success, but absolutely. We do not distinguish ourselves from other individuals but are united to them by our common tragic fate. Appreciation of our life as a whole shares with Spinoza's view from eternity a detachment from finite cares and concerns and with existential agony a submission to mood. But it is neither impersonal and dispassionate nor individualized. Appreciation is personal but not private, compassionate but not anguished.

The compassion that attends appreciation has been, perhaps, the leavening agent within the great traditions of universal religions such as Buddhism and Christianity. The essence of the universal religions is not compassion, but the great religious prophets have incorporated absolute pity into their messages, fringing and framing it with ideas of the sacred, the holy, and ultimate meaning. Divorced from compassion, which it most often is, religion becomes a justification for action, a consolation for failure, and a compensation for frustration and defeat. The principle of compassion, which has never been actualized by any religious institution, is forgive them for they know not what they do. Rather than being based on compassion, religions capture it and subordinate it to plans for salvation or schemes of self-perfection and liberation, taming and containing it within the bounds of convention. They preach that we are capable of knowing what we do and therefore, implicitly or expressly, that we deserve to be punished and are forgiven only through mercy, if, indeed, we are forgiven at all. Compassionate appreciation, then, is not dependent upon a religious mentality or experience but is antithetical to most religious practice. We are capable of spontaneous compassion over life's tragedy without the support of God or ultimate reality, and our pity is all the more acute without such supports.

Absolute pity is beyond all comparative judgments of good and evil. When we appreciate life's structure, we do not struggle to transcend and overcome moral judgment but are removed altogether from its guidance. In the face of life's necessary failure we are stripped of any relative standards of right and wrong, success and defeat, useful and useless. Left without any justification for our conduct, we feel pity about our wretched condition in which fear makes us strive to justify ourselves and thus to separate ourselves from others, to judge them according to their performance, and to compete with them for care and attention. We grasp the necessity of the conventional ego at the same time that we understand its mendacity and thus become aware that knowledge is not virtue, that what is called virtue demands the sacrifice of the essential truth about our lives. No ethical definition of our being can assert that we are fundamentally impractical, that our life is inadequate to itself. Rather, notions of virtue must offer us consistent principles in the name of which we may strive to surmount imperfection or battle against evil. Appreciation has no conceptual or ideal standards but, in their absence, makes a clearing for compassion.

The bond between pity and acknowledgment of our incompletion is not logical but experiential. There is nothing in the concept of incompletion that implies a compassionate attitude toward life. Even from a psychological standpoint, it would be just as plausible for us to respond to our ultimate failure with contempt as with compassion. Much of religious and even atheistic existentialism is in fact based upon contempt for ourselves. In many people, our fragility, dependency, and inadequacy evokes scorn and possibly hatred for our being. We are, for these people, wretched beings who continually devise excuses for their failures and ideals for which they congratulate themselves and then proceed to violate in practice. Northern European philosophies derived from Protestantism are often permeated with such contempt. The mainstream of German idealism from Kant through G.W.F. Hegel masked this contempt by efforts to show that our ideals might be vindicated in practice. The dissenting tradition, particularly in Nietzsche and Kierkegaard, demystified idealism by showing us how wretched we are and then delivered us over to a perpetual effort to transcend ourselves or to a leap of faith. Contempt for our being is rooted in an inability to surrender the practical viewpoint. Both the mainstream idealists and the religious existentialists dwell within the realm of possibility, comparing themselves with an ideal of perfection stressing autonomy and self-sufficiency to which they are inadequate. This ideal is not life's native and contradictory impulse to conscious completion but a consistent standard of obedience to a higher law. Even the dissenters do not escape the idealistic system, counseling obedience to instinct or to revelation.

Appreciation does not result in contempt because it has given up all hope for salvation, thereby also relieving itself of despair. If we understand our failure to be necessitated by the structure of our being and our inadequacy to be irremediable, our ideals to be conventional, and our lives to be internally contradictory, we will not be contemptuous toward ourselves but rather will pity our self-contempt. Compassion is the only attitude that is fully self-referential, because it allows us to accept ourselves as we are, not as we might hope to be. Despair, resentment, and contempt are reactions to disillusionment and are based on the judgment that we have been cheated by life. The existentialists who criticize the crowd mentality so bitterly attribute it to weakness of will, not to a necessary response to betrayal and fear. They call upon us to suffer and to be resolute, ruthlessly ferreting out hypocrisy and leaving us with no comfort in the lies we tell ourselves. But if knowledge is not virtue, we are incapable of living in truth. We will always lie to ourselves and to one another; we cannot do otherwise when we take our actions seriously. At best we can temper the ruthlessness of control with compassion. And if we refuse to take any of our actions seriously and make of life a game or a drama, we deliver ourselves over to the most profound contempt of all, veiling our self-hatred with comedy.

Far closer to the appreciative vision of life than the Northern European idealists and existentialists is Dostoevski, who in *The Brothers Karamazov* offered a striking contrast between compassion and rebellion. The rebel, Ivan Karamazov, is so acutely aware of evil that he sets himself against God, proclaiming his right to decide and to act for himself. If God permits evil, Ivan reasons, He is not worthy of human obedience. In contrast, Father Zossima is guided by a vision of our fundamental continuity with one another and our mutual implication in one another's sins and, therefore, of our responsibility to one another. Although Zossima interprets his vision in terms of Christian symbols, it does not depend upon those symbols to validate it; rather, it is directly intuited. The struggle between the rebellious and compassionate viewpoints is even present in the tortured Ivan's relation of the Legend of the Grand Inquisitor. After the Grand Inquisitor has warned Jesus to leave Spain on pain of death, Jesus does not argue with him or threaten him but kisses him and departs. For Dostoevski, the lesson of our evil is the judgment: forgive them for they know not what they do. This lesson is contradictory to the demands of the practical viewpoint, summarized in the Grand Inquisitor's slogan of miracle, mystery, and authority, and in his notion that human beings need bread and meaning and that they loathe freedom. Dostoevski's insistence upon public confession of crime and voluntary submission to punishment flow from his insight into our basic solidarity and his compassion for our inadequacy to one another. He believed that only through revealing our weakness and insufficiency could we form a community based on our interdependence and not on our separation. Although Dostoevski was perhaps more aware of our depravity than any other thinker, he was not contemptuous of our being but appreciated the yawning want and the need for relations to the world and to others at the core of our life. Ivan saw us as we often hope that we might be—self-sufficient and autonomous, our own lawgivers. Zossima saw us as we are—longing to accept ourselves and in need of pity.

Absolute pity does not detract from our dignity but is the ground of it. When, on the other side of practice, we glimpse our incessant struggles to achieve meaning, the conventional barriers we erect between ourselves and others, our attempts to defend our rights and to gain advantage, and the contradiction of our native ideal, we pity life's inadequacy of itself but we also honor our efforts to overcome fear, even when they are mendacious. For appreciation there is no middle ground between compassion and judgment. Either we acknowledge the tragedy of all life and sympathize with it or we evaluate the quality of lives, judging some better or more significant than others and rating ourselves according to the ideal criterion we have set up. Appreciation is so contrary and dangerous to the practical viewpoint because it equalizes all lives, leveling them with the same pity and honor. Judgment is a variation of control and so is exclusive, selective, and never fully bound over to any experience. Appreciation is inclusive, tempering all of our moral judgments with acknowledgment of tragedy.

## 4. CONCRETE DURATION

Appreciation directed to the present reveals the polemical aspect of our being, our struggle to suspend the practical viewpoint, to loosen the grip of control, and to peer behind the conventional ego's veil. Its terminus is the dissolution of our relations with the world and with others and the recapture of our essential solitude in the nothingness of attention. Appreciation directed toward the future discloses the tragic destiny of our life, its incompletion, and its contradictory aim of conscious completion. Its terminus is absolute pity and insight into our continuity with the struggles and the frustration of all life. The struggle of appreciation against control, one phase of our polemical being, individualizes us by drawing us back to the origins of the practical viewpoint in absolute abandonment and the terror we feel when we are left alone with ourselves. The appreciation of our tragedy universalizes us by uniting us to others in a common fate. Appreciation of the past, the remaining direction of the appreciative motive, personalizes us as unique and concrete individuations of tragic existence.

According to Unamuno, each one of us is a unique species, incorporating within our lives a multitude of selves, some of which have become extinct, others of which have mutated and evolved, and still others of which persist in the present, often confronting one another in bitter conflict.

The expression of these selves, their victories and defeats, and their struggles to become actualized in the practical viewpoint are the substance of our autobiographies. Appreciation of our unique and concrete being involves the recovery of ourselves as unique species primarily by discovering how we have expressed other persons to ourselves and how we have carried forward their hopes into our lives while altering them to accord with our novel experiences, our responses to fear, and the restrictions and opportunities of our social relations. In order to appreciate ourselves as unique species we must break the hold of the conventional ego, which offers us an official autobiography based upon a self-definition adapted to the requirements of social life, particularly the need to secure care and attention from others. We have always expressed far more than our official autobiographies permit us to acknowledge, and we have always repressed possibilities that we still yearn to actualize. For others we are, for the most part, what we do. But for ourselves we are primarily what we have expressed and have been able to appreciate.

Ever since Descartes defined the starting point of philosophy as self-reflection, thinkers have sought to define the subject. From the appreciative viewpoint, subjectivity is not thinking substance but the synthesis of life and awareness in the polemical structure opposing expression to convention. Although the contents of our self-definitions are multiple and disperse us, as Unamuno taught, into many selves, there is but one form of self-activity. We emerge as unique species because life is responsive to itself and to what lies beyond it and does not merely react mechanically to forces that impinge upon it. At least in our lives response is not merely a link in a chain of efficient causation or in a sequence of means to an end but has elements of appreciative self-reference. The most rudimentary form of appreciative self-reference is feeling, which not only impels us to seek completion but is a comment on the state of our being and thus is the origin of our fundamental impracticality. For example, from a medical standpoint, pain is a signal of functional disharmony, while in our ordinary lives it is usually a domination we seek to eliminate or at least to suppress so that we can continue our daily round of tasks. But pain is also a feeling upon which we comment by what we call the experience of suffering. We appreciate pain by suffering it and attending to our suffering, part of which involves our efforts to surmount it, but part of which is merely awareness of the complex of feelings and attitudes itself. Our ability to focus attention upon our feelings, our primal responses to life and its insistent dynamic, allows us to transcend the order of mechanism and to understand ourselves as living beings.

We do not, however, only feel a succession of experiences; we also make judgments upon them through sound and gesture and then become aware of those judgments and, more important, of the fact that we have made them. What I have called expression in the preceding discussion is just this spontaneous gesturing and vocalizing, which adds a running commentary to the flow of sensation and feeling. In order for us to express a response to an event and not only to feel it, our experience must be ordered sufficiently to allow us to appreciate it as a whole. We must experience integrated unities of quality that have been organized without our deliberate control, not merely dispersed sensations and feelings. Our primordial expressions, too, must emerge outside the realm of conscious control and provide the material upon which the motive of control operates. The fundamental self originates in life, not in awareness. Before we are centered in the head we are centered in the heart and breast. The concrete self is an expression of life and exists by virtue of its incompletion. Attention, which in the Greek tradition is the fount of the soul, is no-thing. We vocalize and gesture spontaneously before we learn a language; and language, of course, would not be possible if our life were not inherently expressive.

To the scientific mentality, feeling and expression are mysterious enough, but memory is entirely incomprehensible. Not only do we feel our responses and give a running commentary on them, but we also preserve them and fuse them to one another, again spontaneously. As Justus Buchler noted, we are "summed up selves in process." We do not merely react to each emerging present afresh, deploying our biological equipment to master it momentarily, but we incorporate past judgments into our present response effortlessly, mutating silently and synthesizing a character. We do not merely store information and retrieve it in appropriate circumstances for practical aims, but we actualize a new past in each present. From the very inception of our lives we become "experienced." The cognitive processes of recall and remembrance are but pale reflections of the deeper processes of summation and integration that teach us many lessons that elude our conceptual knowledge. Our first cry of terror is not the same as the ones that follow because we have learned the lesson of betrayal and carry it forward into the future. We are historical beings, not primarily because we project meanings and act to achieve them, but because the growth of experience is intrinsic to life. We are spontaneously traditional, and each one of us has a unique tradition. Collective histories would be inconceivable were life not autobiographical. The ground of group histories is our concrete duration.

Feeling, expression, and memory are the three spontaneous life processes that give us a concrete self and allow us to appreciate. By virtue of their operation we "have experiences" rather than merely undergo them in a blind succession. Our polemical being is grounded in the twin supports of our incompletion, which impels us forward to a contradictory ideal, and our concrete duration, which pulls us backward into the richness of what we have become. What we have become is not fundamentally what we have done in our practical lives but what we have felt, have expressed, and have been able to incorporate into a character. Our character contains much that we have not organized into the conventional ego and that may threaten its consistency and effectiveness and therefore its security. Our responses, for the most part, are not practical and are ill-adapted to our persistence in the symbolic time of past-present-future. We derive pleasure from experiences whose objects disrupt our bodily functions; we fear events that will cause us no material injury; we cherish desires for which others would ostracize us; and we have insights that are subversive of our will to control ourselves and others. Were we not so ill-adapted to practice, we would not have to make such efforts to take care of ourselves, we would not have to create a conventional ego, and we would not find it so difficult to appreciate our life. The irony of control is that although it arises from our impracticality, it forces us to interpret ourselves as practical beings.

We are social beings whose most significant responses are to one another. Our uniquely personal traditions are not created by our own unaided efforts but are initially and throughout our lives based primarily on our expression of others to ourselves. Josiah Royce understood only a small part of our sociality when he observed that we are beings whose destiny is to complete one another's meanings. We not only connect with others because they are sources of ideas that inform us about our goals and the means to them, but we forge deeper bonds rooted in affection. As infants we express others to ourselves as sources of care and attention and then, through the most unfathomable and profound mystery of all, begin to care about them, attend to them, and acknowledge them as sources of expressions that we can reexpress to ourselves. The relations between children and those who nurture them is reciprocal but not symmetrical. The first concern of the elders is to care for, and attend to, the young physically, providing them with what they need to survive, fondling them, and teaching them, primarily through reward and punishment, to take responsibility for their own lives in a specific network of social relations. The children, however, care about, and attend to, the elders appreciatively, watching and listening to their expressions and then repeating them and somehow assimilating not only the meanings that they signify but also the emotions that provoked them. The foundation of our sociality is sympathy, not in the sense that we can think ourselves into another person's situation, but in the sense that the others' expressions *evoke* within us their responses and thus their feelings and even their memories. The elders represent the young by serving their present and future needs, but the young represent the elders by recapitulating their experience and carrying it forward in the stream of life. The young make from the past the present and future, often by actualizing for the first time hopes and desires the elders have suppressed and perhaps officially prohibit.

Our concrete selves are complex blends of our own spontaneous expressions and of the expressions that we have assimilated from others. When we appreciate our past we distinguish among the desires and judgments we have made our own and those that we have merely borrowed so that we might insure the care and attention of others for us. We glimpse desires and fears we have suppressed and judgments we have neglected because they would subvert the tenuous unity of the conventional ego if they were carried forward into practice. Our genuine autobiography unfolds before us and overwhelms our official interpretation of the past, revealing the compromises we have made, the traumas we could not express and would not remember, and most important, all of the hopes and demands we have represented because we feared the withdrawal of care and attention, and sought to win the approval of those upon whom we depended. We also glimpse what we failed to appreciate fully because of the hatred that marked our encounter with betrayal.

Appreciation of our past is also the appreciation of the others whom we have expressed to ourselves. Their unique being, their differences and separation from us, are revealed as we divide what we have made our own from what we have merely borrowed. We glimpse the special ways in which they have experienced life's tragedy, and we are compassionate toward them even though they have wounded us. We appreciate their conflicts and struggles because their expressions have been evocative. They have been essential to us, yet are separate. Despite their physical distance from us in space and symbolic time, their experience exists within us but is never perfectly integrated. We are neither monadic nor continuous with a greater whole but are unique centers of expression who are permeable to others. Our most impressive achievement is not the conventional and individualized self, which is a response to fear; rather, it is our uniquely concrete personality, which grows spontaneously and unbidden but whose fulfillment depends upon the deep love that allows us to accord attention to the expressions of others and to sympathize with them. Appreciation requires receptivity to life, and the perfection of appreciation is receptivity to other lives than our own, our full acknowledgment of each of them as uniquely absolute.

Appreciation of our incompletion leaves us with universal compassion for life, but appreciation of our concrete durational being leaves us with a deeper compassion for each particular life that we have expressed, including our own. As we distinguish our own traditions from those of others we experience a wonder at who we are that counterbalances pity. We are infinitely precious because we are unique centers for expressing life who can never be replaced. Feeling, expression, and memory make us ends in ourselves who transcend any performance of practical functions and the conventional fictions that control us. The tragedy of our concrete being is that our infinite worth overflows the ability of life to support it adequately. Our incompletion wars against our uniqueness; our appreciation is vastly richer than our practical possibilities; our expressions are always more varied and more complex than our self-definitions. Each one of us is absolute and irreplaceable, but each one treats the others as though they were mere elements of social relations. As much as we struggle to appreciate, we are doomed to spend most of our lives in the practical viewpoint, divided from others and from our own pasts and struggling to ward off fear and prevent betrayal. Appreciation makes us receptive to the kingdom of ends, not Kant's realm of self-legislating rational beings, but the present and actual world of unique and concrete persons, who are always with us but whom we never fully acknowledge. Appreciation has no immediate link with action, because action is based on exclusive and meaningful achievements, not on the evocation of experience. At best, the insight gained when we fall under the motive of appreciation can temper our ordinary ruthlessness with compassion.

# CHAPTER IV

# SACRIFICE

Although we may have interludes in which we are able to appreciate the structure of our life and to glimpse ourselves as polemical, incomplete, and uniquely concrete beings, for the most part we are delivered over to the practical viewpoint and are dominated by the motive of control. As it operates in our ordinary existence, the motive of control has no principle but the imperative that we impel ourselves out of the expanded present and into the symbolic past-present-future, which is given content by a meaning. Control lacks principle because it is a response to fear, which is the only response we cannot appreciate because it draws us away from our life by making us concerned with what we will become, careful about the dangers that might assail us, and preoccupied with maintaining our foothold in the world and our standing in social relations. Control itself is sterile with regard to meaning and must be determined by a desire that we have expressed and then made a part of the conventional ego. The contents of the meanings we project into symbolic time are widely diverse, possibly including any of the objects of the desires we have expressed. Which ends are put into the conventional ego depend upon a variety of factors, particularly what we have learned to fear, what has given us pleasure, what we have received from others and expressed to ourselves, and what has drawn our attention away from our essential tragedy and terror before nothingness.

The great question for a philosophy that addresses our life is whether any of the possible determinations of control are in some way better than the others, whether there is a standard for the good life that can be defended. From the standpoint of efficient causation, we can attempt to discover the conditions in which some of all of the possible meanings are incorporated into the conventional ego rather than others. This is and has been the business of sociology and psychology, the former clarifying the structures of social relations that favor some meanings over others, the latter clarifying the processes by which individuals carry forward some meanings into practice and repress or reject others. Philosophy is not concerned with the question of which particular meanings are incorporated into the conventional ego at specific places and times or of why they have been incorporated in the sense of efficient causation, although it is tangent to sociology and psychology when it analyzes the dynamics through which meanings are created. Rather, philosophy seeks to discover which meanings are desirable and then to show why they are so in a sense that is yet to be defined. Philosophy, then, must encounter the problems of ethics and address the perplexities of our practical life in terms of what it has discovered about our life as a whole.

We should not assume that philosophy can resolve the

problem of determining the good. Perhaps good and evil, right and wrong, better and worse, desirable and undesirable are merely relative judgments, all of which are based upon contingent compromises of our native ideal of conscious completion. If so, philosophy has nothing to say about our practical life but that it conceals from us our fundamental being, that it is ultimately vain, that it is predicated upon fear, and that all of its meanings are equal in the sense that they are all inadequate substitutes for the contradictory aim of life. But it is also conceivable that an analysis of our life as a whole, in both its practical and impractical phases, contains at least some clues about how we might conduct ourselves well. Even the bare insight that we are essentially impractical beings who are thrown unwillingly into action tempers our confidence in the absolute worth of any partial and consistent meaning we seek to achieve, fostering skepticism about our congenital self-importance. Certainly, the ethics that might be compatible with a vision of our life that rejects the principle that knowledge is virtue will differ in many respects from ethical systems that are based upon this principle. But the denial that knowledge is virtue, that an adequate cognition can provide standards by which we should limit our conduct, implies neither a denial of knowledge nor a denial of virtue but only of a certain relation of priority between the two.

## ETHICS

The great tradition of Western ethics has been based upon the cognitive fallacy, the idea that through knowledge we can determine what is good for us and then guide our conduct in accordance with that good. There have been endless variations of the cognitive fallacy, depending upon what type of knowledge has been held to reveal the good, how adequate we are to achieving it, and of course its specific content. The constant throughout all of these endeavors has been the belief that we are essentially practical beings who need only to sort out what is intrinsically worthwhile from what only appears to be so in order to lead consistently virtuous lives. The general method of the great tradition has been to select some aspect of our life, to value it above the others, and then to offer maxims concerning how we should or might perfect ourselves. The basis of ethics is, as G. E. Moore noted, not the maxims that are supposed to guide conduct, but the determination of the highest good and its grounds. Even Kant, who concerned himself primarily with clarifying maxims of conduct, based his discussion of imperatives on the assertion that the only good without limitation is a good will. Ethics must be grounded in a notion of goodness because it seeks to inform practice, and practical life is always directed toward the actualization of a meaning. The way we distinguish among meanings in practical life is by judging them comparatively according to their worthiness as objects for commitment, and ethical inquiry seeks to provide criteria for our judgments.

The variations of the cognitive fallacy are familiar to those who have undertaken even a superficial study of the history of philosophy. Systematic ethics began in ancient Greece under the sign of reason. The Greek philosophers, beginning with Socrates and Plato, initiated the tradition of natural law, which is founded on the idea that by understanding our nature through critical reflection upon our judgments we can arrive at universally valid cognitions of the ends we should seek and the principles of relation that make the achievement of those ends possible. According to the natural law tradition, the good is objective and consistent and, most important, intelligible to reason purified of conflicting opinions conditioned by the flux of sensation. For the Greeks and their followers what reason apprehends is a harmony of our functions, the norm of which is the idea of justice. The Greek tradition was later supplemented and disrupted by Judaeo-Christian ethics based on the authority of revelation that prescribed the rejection of finite harmony, justice, and happiness in favor of obedience to absolute commandments and sacrificial love. Throughout the medieval period Greek harmony and Christian sacrifice, reason and revelation, provided the themes for philosophers engaged in ethical inquiry, who attempted to reconcile the conflicting ideals and orders of knowledge. However, regardless of the tension between, or even outright incompatibility of, the ideal of Athens and that of Jerusalem, the principle that knowledge is virtue remained intact. Whether the knowledge proceeded from unaided reason purified of circumstantial determination or from the will of God revealed in holy books, it was considered to be regulative over conduct.

Modern subjectivism, which challenged both the Greek notion of objective teleology and the authority of revelation, did not reject the cognitive fallacy. Utilitarians identified the good with sensation and counseled instrumentally rational conduct to achieve a maximum of pleasure or happiness, however they might be defined and refined by different thinkers. Kant and his followers identified the good with volition, criticizing the utilitarians for failing to transcend the order of inclination and to reflect upon the will itself, purged of all of its sensual determinations. Naturalists renewed the Greek tradition but substituted for rational reflection upon our judgments the methods of science and its conclusions about our behavior.

At the turn of the twentieth century, G. E. Moore challenged modern subjectivism in the name of objective intuition. He critiqued the naturalistic fallacy, which he defined as the principle that the good can be defined conceptually, arguing instead that the good is an undefinable quality, no different in that respect from colors and sounds. Yet Moore, who devastated the great tradition of Western ethics, stopped short of renouncing the cognitive fallacy. Even if we could not define the good in terms of something else, we could still know it intuitively and make correct judgments about its presence or absence in situations. He even argued that we are obliged to strive to actualize the good in cases in which no human being would be able to appreciate it, just because the good is intrinsically valuable and the universe is better for containing more of it.

The cognitive fallacy, then, permeates nearly all of the Western ethical tradition and makes it decidedly dogmatic. The tradition is, in fact, a nest of dogmatisms, each one of them conflicting with the others and each one denying us some of our most cherished and deeply rooted possibilities, reducing them to mere appearance or outright evil. Dogmatism in ethics may proceed from any type of knowing, as rational, revealed, empirical, and intuitive ethical systems have amply demonstrated. Ethical dogmatism is based on the assumption, never criticized by anyone who works within the great tradition, that the good is adequate to the demand of our practical life for a consistent meaning that

we can project into the past-present-future and then strive
to achieve by bringing ourselves and the world under control. If, however, we are not essentially practical beings and
in addition are fundamentally contradictory, no knowledge
of whatever sort can provide us with consistent prescriptions for a virtuous life.

Opposition to the dogmatic tradition in ethics has not,
most often, been based upon a critical description of our
life but upon a logical denial of cognitivism. The most
recent forms of skepticism have been "noncognitivist," rejecting the claim that we can achieve conceptual knowledge of the good and endeavoring to clarify what we do, in
fact, mean when we engage in moral discourse. The ethical
skeptics have argued most frequently that when we use
such terms as "good" and "evil" we are actually attempting
to persuade others to accept our own particular preferences, which arise from our reflection upon our desires. The
good, then, is merely the desired, not the desirable, and
there is no objective obligation attached to its attainment.
For the ethical skeptic the "good" is merely one of the
many weapons we deploy to control one another in social
life, having the instrumental value, at least, of being inex-
pensive in comparison with other means such as force,
threat, and bribery. If we are able to persuade others that
some deed is intrinsically worthy or that they have an
obligation to perform it, we need expend no more effort or
resources to get them to meet our expectations and to
provide us with the particular kinds of care and attention
we desire.

Ethical skepticism is not merely an academic theory divorced from the practical viewpoint but a description of
the principles of social relations when they have been

brought fully under the motive of control. The skeptical attitude is most conspicuously present, not in intellectual discourse, which attenuates it and makes it benign by suggesting the ways in which people may reach a consensus of opinion, but in the activities of business and government. The academic skeptics blunt the worship of control that grounds their claims by insisting that we understand that good and evil, right and wrong, are nonsense words. Presumably, if we understand that moral discourse is just a fig leaf with which we disguise the nudity of our preferences, we will not be taken in by the exhortations of others, and even more important, we will temper our own absolute claims and become more humble about our demands and therefore more responsible and civil. The academic skeptic is just as caught up in the cognitive fallacy as the dogmatist. In this case, the great hope is that we will not be fanatical and violent if we are deprived of our justifications. Knowledge still means virtue even when virtue proceeds from knowing that we cannot speak sensibly about it.

The lesson of the academic skeptics is of course lost on their practical counterparts. The most characteristic intellectual invention of the twentieth century has not been any advance in technical philosophy but advertising and propaganda. The manipulators of mass opinion take seriously the idea that the notion of a supreme good is meaningless, but they are also aware that belief in such a good can be useful to them. Hence, unlike the academic skeptics, advertisers and propagandists seek to keep people from the knowledge that moral discourse is meaningless and instead attempt, through the most sophisticated means they can devise, to persuade people that there is indeed a supreme good and that they are obliged to pursue it in particular ways. The principle of advertising and propaganda, then, is the big lie, while the principle of academic skepticism is that the truth makes us free. Academic skepticism, however, has no grounds for advancing the proposition that it is better to tell the truth than to lie, better to know the truth than to deceive oneself or to allow oneself to be deceived. Advertisers and propagandists are just as consistent with noncognitivism as are their academic foes. Their principle, as Dostoevski understood, is that nothing is forbidden and therefore that everything is possible. The academic skeptics respond that moral discourse is meaningless and therefore that mendacity is forbidden.

At the root of the contradiction between intellectual skepticism and its practical counterpart is a struggle over power and control. The practical skeptics, the advertisers and propagandists, have all the advantage on their side, because they have access to the mass media of communication and the resources of the vast organizations that regulate our daily lives. They are free to act in the name of increased organizational control, limited only by competing conglomerates and the critical acuity of their subject populations. The academic skeptics desperately and pathetically seize upon the possibility that people might learn to become more self-critical and attempt to make them so through rational persuasion, marshaling the scant resources of university presses and scholarly journals and control over the classroom to their worthy end. They are, of course, pitifully unequal to the struggle and become the unwitting and unwilling handmaidens of their foes.

The actual consequences of academic skepticism, particularly in the classroom, contradict, for the most part, the intentions of its advocates. Rather than learning rational humility—the supreme virtue of skepticism and its lasting contribution to our life—the more aggressive students conclude that talk is cheap, that social life is a power struggle, and that they are permitted to get away with anything for which they have the means, since there is no true meaning for existence. The weaker and more frightened students learn that whenever anyone wishes to impose something on them verbally they can defend themselves by stating that they have their own opinions or, more frequently and inconsistently, that they have a right to their own opinions. Sensitive students, who are neither aggressive nor weak, often adopt a cynical detachment, concluding that they are best off absenting themselves from power struggles and leading their own private lives according to personal moral standards. The failure of academic skepticism in the classroom, the only place in which it has a chance of succeeding at all, is a result, not only of the organizational culture that it must combat, but more deeply of its own internal contradiction. If moral discourse is just a cover for the advancement of interest or the ejaculation of emotions, then the imperative to live in the truth is arbitrary. The academic skeptic cannot demonstrate rationally that clarity is better than mendacity and thus must rely upon inspiring appeals to rational humility. Yet the attitude of rational humility is perhaps the virtue least well adapted to moral enthusiasm. The academic skeptics, despite their normally measured, cool, and civilized bearing, are quixotic figures in disguise. They seek to revive the gentlemanly ideal of nineteenth-century bourgeois society in an age of mass manipulation of symbols. They are the Anglo-American equivalents of the more passionate Continental defenders of aristocratic virtue and critics of the masses.

All of the many skeptical tendencies in twentieth-century thought, even those that stop short of noncognitivism (e.g., the various forms of relativism, pragmatism, and existentialism), are rooted in an admirable opposition to contemporary fanaticism, fraud, and manipulation. Confronted with cynical appeals to absolute value, particularly those of fascism, the skeptics and their relatives sought to oppose power with reason, practice with thought, deliverance with personal responsibility. They nursed the radical hope that if we only understood the bankruptcy of all of our ideals we would not be led into evil by demogogues pandering to our basest desires and justifying them by noble proclamations. They interpreted the crisis of our age as the blatant rationalization of passion and resentment and believed that our greatest public need was to deflate our pretensions and to lower our voices. They slew the idealist dragon, the Absolute, urging us to excise the ideal dimension from our lives. Ideals, they believed, are too dangerous for us to entertain. We are far better off if we acknowledge our limitations; realize that our interests are partial, though exhaustive of our possibility; and live with the knowledge of our boundary conditions, whether they are interpreted as the unconscious, social position, cultural particularity, contingent emotion and interest, or finitude. The sacrifice of the ideal dimension, however, is doomed to failure because it requires too massive a surgery on our life, which in one of its essential phases is directed toward an ideal.

Just as Kant recognized the lasting contribution of Hume's skepticism to the theory of knowledge and sought to reconcile this contribution with our demand for objective truth, so we must acknowledge the contribution of contemporary ethical skepticism to the good life while re-

jecting its extreme claim that moral discourse is meaningless. Skepticism embraced the strategy of fighting the
raging fire of cynical demagoguery with the wavering flame
of doubt. For the absolute it substituted the relative, forgetting that relativity is merely a pale reflection of vital dependency. For certainty it substituted ambiguity and
methodical doubt, forgetting that cognitive uncertainty is
but an attenuated form of our polemical being. For salvation it substituted absurdity, forgetting that our rational
demand for unity is but one expression of our deeper longing for conscious completion. And finally, for ideality it
substituted preference, forgetting that each particular, limited, and partial claim is but an expression of a uniquely
concrete being of potentially infinite worth to itself. Skepticism deprived us of our dignity in order to save us from the
consequences of our fear. We could not be betrayed if we
already expected the worst. And the skeptics knew whereof
they spoke, because so many experienced and continue to
experience the worst. Behind skepticism is the painful
awareness of concentration camps, genocide, mass slaugh-
ter, pillage and pollution of the environment, rampant
greed and mistrust, and desolating terror. Skepticism is
neither the cause nor the symptom of our woeful public
situation, but it is the only antibody against it that we have
yet discovered.

A critical ethics, which rejects dogmatic definitions of
the good and still does not reduce moral discourse to a
symbolic game expressing only our interests, preferences, or
passing emotions, must be grounded in the structure of our
being. From a vitalistic standpoint, the notion of goodness
is not derived from reflection upon the possibilities for
action that we contemplate, from a judicious review of the

experiences that we undergo, or from an inquiry into the structure of our choices, but from a description of life's inner dynamic. We are beings who inherently pursue the good by virtue of our being, and we cannot deny our pursuit reflectively but only by negating life through the act of suicide. Life has its own innate ideal, the conscious completion of itself, which differs from the standards of all ethics based upon the cognitive fallacy because it is contradictory and therefore cannot be achieved. G. E. Moore was correct in holding that the good is revealed by intuition but erred when he asserted that this intuition is of a simple quality rather than of the structured dynamic of life itself. The skeptics have been correct to challenge the idea that the good is a consistent and objective standard but have erred in confusing the desirable with the desired. The good is simply an ideal, but it is a peculiar and unique one that is neither a clear and distinct object of intellection nor a simple and separable object of intuition. Both dogmatism and skepticism arise from the mistake of assuming that the good is something that we discover within our life and that stands in a special relation of priority to its other aspects rather than the very direction of life itself.

Life's native ideal of a conscious completion of itself, a resolved synthesis of life and awareness, is analogous to a Kantian a priori in that it is formative of our experience and not a result of our encounters in the world. Each particular and partial meaning we project into the symbolic past-present-future is but a more or less unsatisfactory substitute for the supreme good that we shall never achieve. There is a multitude of finite and possible goods but only one supreme good that overflows all of them and stands as a merciless critic of each of our accomplishments and fulfillments. The ideal of conscious completion is the vitalistic and critical counterpart of the traditional notion of a plenitude or a fullness of life, but critical philosophy acknowledges the internal contradiction of plenitude and thus does not interpret it as a state of being toward which our action can be directed but as a yearning that countervails against and disturbs any complacency we may experience as a result of our efforts in practical existence. The native ideal of life lies on the impractical side of our being, prior to fear and betrayal, both of which make us prudent and stir us to seek comfort and security in symbolic representations of superior forces to which we can deliver ourselves, or in images of consistent and attainable meanings. The great tradition of Western ethics has its back turned to the past and looks in anxious anticipation toward the future, lulling us into forgetfulness of our tragic destiny.

The conscious completion of life is impossible because although the essence of life is to strive to complete itself, that very striving reveals its inherent incompletion. What we call human being is that being in which life has become aware of itself. Awareness of life means both awareness of its dependency on what lies beyond it, its contingency, and its limitation, and also of its inner effort to surmount and overcome these marks of its incompletion. The ideas of incompletion and completion have been treated abstractly and have been given no specific content in the preceding discussion. Every philosophy has a fundamental term or set of terms that cannot be fully analyzed and that, instead, are illustrated by their relation to other analyzable terms. Here the fundamental terms are life, its incompletion, and its struggle to complete itself. What constitutes completion for life cannot be defined according to objective and consistent standards, because such standards can never reflect any more than a selection, always arbitrary, of one or more of life's possibilities. We are completed by anything that we can express to ourselves, and the only thing we cannot express, but can only allude to through our response of terror or resignation, is our loss of relations, our solitude, pure attention, nothingness. Plenitude would be the expression and appreciation of all of our possibilities, actualized fearlessly. A complete life would be one in which life was so bound over to its multitudinous relations, so affirmative of itself, that it would exist in an eternal present. Yet were it to remain life it would have to be ceaselessly moving on, encountering novelty and expanding its expressive responses, deepening and complexifying its uniquely concrete being, and remaining unresolved and unfinished. The unsoundable abyss of life is want, and as long as there is want there is incompletion.

Life, then, is hopelessly antinomic in a variety of related ways. The polemical structure of our being is most deeply rooted in life's internal contradictions. Our struggle to express ourselves completely, to actualize a plenitude of life, runs counter to our particularity, the evidence for which is our concrete duration that gives us an autobiography. Want itself is antinomic, being both the impetus that allows us to live and the goad to its own satiation and therefore to its elimination. In order to live we must will to be perpetually unsatisfied at the same time that we strive for satisfaction. The tensions within our being are compounded after our experience of fear, betrayal, and abandonment. We then move beyond the mere expression of life's responses to the world, others, and itself, and into the effort to control ourselves and our circumstances so that we can carry ourselves, as individuals doomed to care for, and attend to, ourselves, from one present into the next. The motive of control conceals life's inherent contradiction, overlaying it with symbolic substitutes for conscious completion. Yet these substitutes, what we call meanings, are not the results of cognitive error or of misunderstanding but are necessary responses to fear. But we are never fully secure in our conventional meanings and self-definitions and overthrow them in a permanent revolution, despite our attempts to cling to them. As the psychiatrists have shown, we never fully succeed in our attempts to control ourselves and are continually assailed by nightmares, slips of the tongue, phobias, fantasies, resentments, regrets, depressions, and hatreds. We never tie up our loose ends.

The structure of our life is at variance with our most wondrous symbolic achievement, art. The essence of art is not to provide, as do science and philosophy, meanings that help to maintain us in the practical viewpoint, but concrete and individualized resolutions of life. Drama, music, fiction, poetry, painting, sculpture, and dance gain our spontaneous allegiance because they present to us a possible completion of some phase or aspect of our life. They draw us into an expanded present, in which we witness and participate in a finite analogue to our infinite longing. Our life never has the order and meaning of a novel; our movements at work, play, or even in love never actualize the grace of a dance; and our passions never achieve the harmony inherent in the resolution of a chord. The distance of art from life is indicated by the artifice that irreducibly marks any work of the creative imagination or its performance. The artist may strive to achieve the appearance of spontaneous expression, but the work must be calculated to produce an effect and thus must be contained within an ideal form on pain of its dissolving into the everyday. However, when art becomes mere formalism and each work is meant only as an example of the application of rules, it loses our allegiance because it responds to nothing but the intellect. And mathematics and logic serve the intellect far more adequately than arbitrary rules for generating artifacts.

We cannot find the supreme good in art or even in aesthetic experience because they are respites from life's insistent struggle to complete itself. The most profoundly fulfilling experiences that we have, particularly the act of love, combine the concrete symbolism of art with our intimate participation in the creation of a present. They involve neither the mere discharge of drive nor the vicarious witness of a partial completion but a synthesis of the two. Sexual love, to choose the paradigmatic case, is neither the occasion for the release of tension, which would be lust, nor a ritualized drama, which would make the lovers mere examples of social types, but a complete experience uniting the art of seduction and the immediate pleasure of caring and being cared for, attending to and being attended. Short of love, friendship, with all of its occasions for uniting the physical and symbolic dimensions of care and attention, is the crowning achievement of our mutual and interdependent existence, because it overcomes fear and suspicion and allows us to appreciate one another as uniquely concrete beings. In friendship conventions are adapted not to our insecurity but to our interest in allowing the others to overcome their fears. The principle of love and friendship is trust, which is the only motive that allows us to surmount those expressions of control that arise from betrayal. Yet even love and friendship, which are the closest approximations we can achieve to conscious completion, are never adequate to life's contradictory and native ideal. We only love fully and deliver ourselves to trustful friendship when we have appreciated the moral predicament that our life has created for us.

At the root of our moral predicament is a decision, the dimensions or parameters of which are prior to ethical categories. When we withdraw from the practical viewpoint by suspending the motive of control and by allowing ourselves to fall under the guidance of appreciation, we may repeat the mood of anguished terror in which we first resolved to be practical and to separate ourselves from others by taking charge of our own life. If we let ourselves be drawn back toward the nothingness of attention, witnessing our life recede and our relations to the world, others, and ourselves dissolve, we may become aware that although life is united to attention spontaneously in our being, we must participate actively in maintaining this synthesis. At such moments, when we are suspended between life and vicarious death, we may understand that maintaining life requires an affirmation, that we cannot take our existence for granted but must choose to affirm it as it actually is or to deny it. A moment of decision, in which we grasp the either/or choice between the affirmation and denial of life arises only under the condition that we have overcome our basic fear sufficiently not to be thrown automatically back under the domination of the motive of control. The experience of fundamental decision, then, is rare, cannot be planned for, and may be cultivated only imperfectly.

The decision to affirm life or to deny it, the most fundamental choice that it is possible for us to make, is irrational, having no cognitive principle to regulate it. The choice is made, of course, in the light of knowledge about our being, but it is that very knowledge that creates the predicament rather than resolving it. We glimpse ourselves as incomplete, polemical, and concrete beings, who are fated to respond to fear by disguising our actual dynamic and destiny from ourselves. We feel compassion for ourselves but from that compassion draw no grounds for affirming ourselves as we are or for negating our being. We cannot even claim that our decision is free, because freedom has no meaning for us unless it is relative to a choice structured by a standard. Yet we also cannot assert that the decision is determined, because we experience it as flowing out of our own determination and not out of causes that lie beyond our inner dynamic. We interpret our decision in terms neither of final cause nor of efficient cause but in terms of an inexplicable inner necessity, which still is not gratuitous or arbitrary.

The decision to affirm or negate life is not prudential, because the calculation of costs and benefits occurs within the practical viewpoint and results from the choice we have made, either implicitly or expressly. The denial of life does not mean suicide, which may be a sacrificial affirmation of our being, but the surrender to fear and the separation of ourselves from others. Similarly, the affirmation of life does not mean abandonment to concern with perpetuation in the symbolic future, which is most often a pitiful response to fear, but the struggle to overcome fear, to strive to live in acute awareness of our being, to criticize all of our partial meanings in terms of life's native ideal, and to intensify our relations to the world and most important to others. The affirmation of life, then, includes an acceptance

of its incompletion and its finitude, its dependence upon
what lies beyond it, its partiality and enslavement to symbolic time, and its inherent contradiction. It requires that
we acknowledge ourselves simultaneously as uniquely concrete beings of infinite worth and as mere species beings
who are organized causally and functionally into greater
wholes. In the affirmation of life we take full responsibility
for ourselves, not in the sense that we resolve to become
independent of others, but in the sense that we resolve to
fight the battles of our polemical being ourselves, seeking
no substitutes to go to war for us.

The denial of life has multitudinous forms, all of which
are grounded in the separation of ourselves from our relations to the world, others, and ourselves that we achieve
when we fall under the domination of the motive of control. Perhaps the most extreme form of denial is the mysticism of the void, which continually courts the nothingness
of pure attention, making of our life a preparation for, and
a reconciliation with, our death. The mysticism of the void
is the antithesis of life's native ideal of conscious completion, the ideal of plenitude or of a fullness of life. The
mystic of the void interprets life as a veil of appearance, a
wheel of pain, to which the only desirable response is
detachment. Although the mystic may be compassionate
toward others and act charitably, such ethical conduct is
undertaken only to gain liberation from desire. The mystic,
then, does not transcend the practical viewpoint but per-
fects it, ruthlessly eliminating all attempts to control circumstances and attending only to self-control. The object of
self-control and, implicitly, the object of all control is
peace, rest, stasis, what the Stoics called *ataraxia*. Epictetus, the slave philosopher, encapsulated the denial of life

in his famous dictum to suppress concern with any occurrence that we cannot control. Epictetus was certainly the most consistent and thorough of those who have denied life in favor of the separate self, because he concluded that the only occurrence that we can control with certainty is our response to occurrences. For the mystic the response that we cultivate is negative, to be unperturbed either by pleasure or pain, desire or fear, life or death.

The mysticism of the void reveals the limit of the denial of life, the turning of life against itself so that it can be unconcerned with itself. Other forms of denial stop short of the perfection of control and temper self-control with the symbolic expression of some hope. Perhaps the most prevalent form of denial in the modern West is deliverance to Hobbes's ceaseless search for power after power. Those who are so consumed by fear that they interpret life merely as a struggle for survival spend their lives in the pursuit of the means required to undertake action. They strive to amass property, not to use it or enjoy it; to project an image of strength so that others will not harm them; to flatter others so that they will not threaten them; to rely on themselves so that they will not have to depend on others. Life is so dangerous for them, it has betrayed them so often or so deeply, that they will never be secure enough to rest. They do indeed spin perpetually on the mystic's wheel of pain, and so consumed by anxious anticipation are they, so far removed from appreciation, that their only salvation would be the mystic's denial. The great interest in Eastern religions and their coupling with popular psychologies preaching self-reliance in recent years may be explained by an intensification of the war of all against all in contemporary society, the collapse of symbolic and collective systems of ultimate meaning, and the consequent spread of suspicion and mistrust throughout all institutions. The root of denial is the judgment that we must care for, and attend to, ourselves; that we cannot trust others to care for us. The root of this judgment is a sense that we have been betrayed by life and a resentful reaction against betrayal, a protest against having been born as an incomplete being with a contradictory and impossible ideal. While the mystic seeks to do without life itself, the power seeker merely strives to do without the voluntary care and attention of others.

The least obvious and most mendacious forms of denial are those in which life is justified and supported by a meaning the person serves. Whether the meaning is derived from revelation, historical projection, an idea of duty, or a hierarchy of values, its function is to be a substitute for life's native ideal of conscious completion. The great tradition of Western philosophy has been a constant effort to deny life by justifying it and regulating it, by proposing a meaning for it that can be known in an adequate cognition. If we stake our lives on a meaning, we no longer value ourselves as we are but become instruments to something more worthy than ourselves, something that interposes itself between ourselves and others. We become mere materials for the realization of an idea that can never express the richness of our possibility, never reflect back to us the fulfillment of our primal and contradictory demand. There are few mystics among us and not many power seekers. Those who have surrendered themselves to a meaning are legion, and all of them have denied life.

If we affirm life in a resolute and groundless decision, we are thrust into a moral predicament. The affirmation of life requires that we encounter ourselves and one another as polemical, concrete, and incomplete beings, subject to fear and separation, incapable of satisfaction, uniquely and absolutely valuable, but dependent upon one another. Our moral predicament has no resolution but only a structured agony that leaves us ever in doubt and responsible to choose. Our basic moral dilemma, which is repeated each time we act, is which of the absolute lives we should sacrifice and which ones we should enhance. If each life is absolute, each one irreplaceable, each one seeking conscious completion, then no concept or definition or meaning can justify the sacrifice of any one of them. Yet our appreciation is severely limited by our partiality, our unique autobiography, not to mention the conventional ego, which encourages us to feel justified in sacrificing those whom we believe may betray us. Action is always exclusive. Even if we enjoyed an economy of abundance in which all participated, care and attention would be scarce resources, because our attention is always focused. The sense that we are always sacrificing ourselves and others, and that our sacrifices have no justification, yet are necessary, is the moral predicament and the moral motive.

The denial of life saves us from the agony of sacrifice by teaching us that our action can be justified, that our life itself is a betrayal, and that it should or can be redeemed by transcending it, exploiting it, or transforming it to accord with a consistent and ideal image. The affirmation of life is also a refusal to interpret life as a betrayal and at the same time a refusal to interpret it as an opportunity to transcend, exploit, or transform it, each of which is a response to betrayal. We never succeed in affirming life fully, because it is contradictory and subject to fear; but we can, if guided by the appreciation of sacrifice, struggle to overcome fear and, especially, to relax the control generated by denial so that we can become receptive to trust and become loyal to one another. Trust and loyalty are special and limited suspensions of control by which we most fully affirm our being.

## 2. TRUST

The awareness of sacrifice does not provide a conceptual standard by which we can guide our action but a context in which our projects and choices are illuminated and our practical certitude is tempered. It offers us an interpretation of the practical viewpoint derived from appreciation that does not allow us to avoid the necessity of controlling ourselves, others, and circumstances but that makes all of our efforts to control partial, relative, and most of all ultimately unsatisfactory. To know that we always appreciate more than we can reflect in a symbolic meaning, that however generous we may be toward our possibilities we always arbitrarily limit them, and that we are, for the most part, denying life by reacting automatically to fear evokes in us a passionate humility, a compassion that acknowledges but tempers the ruthlessness of action. Passionate humility is not the cool and theoretical humility of the academic skeptic, which leaves us alone with our desires, emotions, and preferences, but a spur to overcome fear and to express others to ourselves. The academic skeptic professes that our life is merely an aggregation of feelings, desires, and cognitions, each of which is a unit that may, at most, be related to the others in a hierarchical order of preference. For the skeptic, then, sacrifice may be an aspect of life, but it is not, as it is for the vitalist, definitive of life itself and revelatory of its essential structure.

The awareness of sacrifice does not guarantee that any specific good will be sought, any particular possibility projected, or any specific principle applied, but only that no good, possibility, or value will be interpreted as a justification for life. Life itself, when it has been affirmed in its fullness and appreciated compassionately, is its own justification. We begin to seek guarantees of life's meaning, the goodness of being, or the necessary fulfillment of our yearnings only when we do not or cannot affirm ourselves as we are, when we flee from acknowledgment of our absolute worth as uniquely concrete beings and of our essential incompletion. Life is sacrificial because each one of us is a center for expressing and appreciating experience who needs the care and attention of others in order to express. Our primary relation to the world is to express one another to ourselves, which implies that others must exercise sufficient forbearance to care for, and attend to, us. They must not seek to control us so fully that we become images of their partial lives, mere instruments for confirming their self-definitions, or predictable variables in their experiments to maintain control and independence. Each time we separate ourselves from others and undertake to manipulate them in accordance with a concealed design we are depriving them of the possibility of expressing us in their own lives and therefore are breaking the primary social bond. Yet we continually conceal and manipulate because we lack trust. We believe that honest expression of ourselves to others will cause them to fear us or take advantage of our weaknesses. Not only are we expressive. We are also vulnerable and subject to fear.

The greatest sacrifice we can make is to trust another human being. By trust is not meant the superficial confidence in others that we often have in everyday life and that is based upon our implicit or express belief that others are under control either because they have surrendered themselves to a symbolic meaning or have been effectively disciplined by external threat. Such trust is merely a practical sense of security, which is delusive because if we thought clearly enough we would know that fear is the most fragile of bonds, always ready to come apart when it is displaced by a greater fear or by an overmastering desire. The deceptive character of what ordinarily passes for trust is indicated by our ceaseless attempts to verify that it is well grounded. We continually check out our associates to determine whether they are still under control, whether their commitments are weakening, whether they remain sufficiently meek; and if we detect a problem we take remedial measures, either threatening or encouraging them to comply with our expectations. Often we are not aware of how much effort we expend keeping up the social compact, which is primarily a defensive alliance. The supreme good of defensive society is the transient comfort we feel when we witness others discharging their duties conventionally and automatically. This is, perhaps, the peace that Hobbes made the goal of political activity. Such peace requires that we present ourselves to one another as fictions and functions, not as uniquely concrete and spontaneous beings who are impelled by a contradictory ideal and are capable of surprising us.

A deeper trust than the confidence we feel when others are under control involves the voluntary suspension of our efforts to control them and, therefore, a sacrifice of our independence, self-reliance, and efforts to insure that our own symbolic meanings will be actualized. So long as we stake our lives upon a partial meaning projected into the symbolic past-present-future, we cannot trust others because we will be striving to make sure that they cooperate with us or at least do not disturb or threaten us. They will recede into our physical circumstances, becoming part of the scenery and losing their unique individuality. Genuine trust requires not only that we give others some leeway in certain respects within a system of "ordered liberty" but that we resolutely decenter ourselves and choose the other's concrete being over any accomplishment of our own or of a group. We must, in short, resolve that the other be more important within our own lives than any symbolic meaning that we project.

The paradox of trust is that we make the other more significant to us than any of our possible achievements primarily through forbearance. It is by abstaining from control that we open up a clearing in which others may express themselves to us and, therefore, in which we can express them to ourselves. Trust does not mean leaving others alone to go about their private business, as the classical liberals had it, but according attention to them and providing them with care. Perhaps no philosopher has understood trust better than Martin Heidegger, who based authentic relations with others upon solicitude. Heidegger called what is here termed trust "leaping ahead" and contrasted it with "leaping in." When we "leap ahead" of others we attempt to appreciate their unique autobiographies and draw from them the possibilities that overcome fear. We may try to create the conditions in which those possibilities can be brought forward into action, but we do not become substitutes for the others. Such substitution, in which we lead the others' lives for them, either by representing the possibilities they will not or cannot actualize themselves, or by intervening physically to solve their problems, is "leaping in." For Heidegger, the negation of solicitude is indifference, which, as the preceding discussion has shown, is based upon the superficial everyday confidence that the other is harmless.

Instances of trust occur throughout our lives and are most often transient suspensions of control actuated by appreciation of the other's uniquely absolute existence. In order to sustain trust over symbolic time we must not limit it merely to those expanded presents in which we are swept away by compassion, enthusiasm, and generosity, but must project it as a meaning. Trust in another that is projected into the symbolic past-present-future is loyalty. We are loyal to the other when we do not allow the betrayals that necessarily occur with frequency to throw us into resentment and self-reliance and to abandon our disposition to attend and to care. If we allow loyalty to be reflected in our conventional ego, we are bound over to an effort not to let betrayal impel us to separate ourselves from the other. We have absolute worth and so does the other, and we are mutually inadequate to one another's demands for conscious completion. We will, then, always fail and disappoint one another. Genuine loyalty is undertaken in full awareness of its fragility and is not supported by prudential calculations or absolute imperatives, both of which separate us from the other's terrifying absolute reality. When we are loyal to other persons, we understand that they are as agonized and incomplete as we are; that they are capable of betraying us so deeply that we will not, whatever be our wishes, be able to trust them again; that they may abandon us and therefore make a joke out of our past deliverance to them. Yet if we affirm life we really have no other choice but to be loyal to the particular others who depend on us and upon whom we depend, who express our lives as we express theirs.

Trust and loyalty are not universal imperatives but are voluntary commitments undertaken by concrete persons toward particular others in specific circumstances. We cannot trust and be loyal to individuals whom we have not expressed to ourselves, except in an attenuated sense of providing some physical care and attention to them or offering them cultural objects we have created. Further, trust and loyalty are not altruistic but depend upon mutuality. If we try to make of our lives sacrifices to others, we deny our own absolute worth and become mere projections of the others' demands. Even in Christianity we are told to love our neighbors as ourselves. And, as Unamuno noted, if we do not love ourselves how can we love our neighbors? Perhaps we should honor Jesus for revealing that the essence of our life is sacrifice, but we should not imitate Christ.

Devotion to others in trust and loyal commitment to them require that we acknowledge and affirm our being as it is revealed to us when we are guided by the motive of appreciation. In relations of mutual loyalty persons seek to place the care of the conventional ego in the others so that they can express the others to themselves and suspend defensive self-control. From the side of the one who is trusted, opportunities open up for spontaneous expression of desires, admission of fears and weaknesses, recovery of repressed traumas, and experimentation with new and challenging projects. The other becomes one to whom confidences may be directed, and the expression of confidences enhances the person's confidence. The one who is trusted gives the others access to a unique autobiography, which in turn deepens their appreciation of the possibilities of life. Through expression unclouded by defense people come to understand themselves better and to determine their own finite destinies in accordance with the possibilities that grow out of their concrete duration, out of the past they have made present by exposing it to the light of publicity and criticism. Only abstractly can we speak of an absolute freedom in which nothing is forbidden and everything is possible, and in which we can revoke our past commitments. As concrete durational beings, each one of us distinguishes among live and dead options, our judgments being based upon whom we have represented, what has been permitted to us, and how we have been limited by betrayal. The friend, the one who has accorded trust to us, knows, often better than we do, which of our options are live and which ones dead, which ones will challenge us to overcome fear and which ones will cast us back into resentful abandonment, and which ones will allow us to express others more fully to ourselves. As we are accorded trust by the others, we in turn trust their judgments about us, allowing their advice, encouragement, and warnings to enter into the context in which we make our decisions.

From the side of the one who trusts, life becomes a struggle to overcome suspicion and to take risks. When we accord trust to another person, we risk both being betrayed and betraying. Perhaps the other will violate our confidences, take advantage of our vulnerability, fail to provide us with care and attention, or try to make us dependent and therefore pliable. Perhaps we will not control ourselves sufficiently to forbear from rejecting the other or will succumb to the temptation to separate ourselves and seek our own advantage. Trust is so difficult because it reverses the native tendency of the practical viewpoint toward independence and binds self-control to appreciation of the other's expressions and not to what they indicate for the success of our own projects. The other person is not a meaning that remains constant while we vary our efforts to achieve it, but a concrete being who is continually mutating and is always capable of surprising us. We may become disillusioned of our meanings when we discover that their actualization does not fulfill our hopes for them, but we cannot be betrayed by meanings. Only other persons can betray us, which may account for why we so desperately seek security in the nonhuman and the invariant. Even Josiah Royce, who founded his ethics upon loyalty, believed that the supreme principle of morality was loyalty to the idea of loyalty, not loyalty to other particular and incomplete beings. Royce's "loyalty to loyalty" is yet another variation on the motive of control, providing each of us with an ideal incentive to continue to trust one another despite betrayal and fallibility. Only by abjuring such ideal and symbolic supports do we encounter directly and immediately that which is most real to us, our *effective* reality, the other person.

The ethics of sacrifice, trust, and loyalty is in sharp contrast to Sartre's existentialist ethics. For Sartre, others are hell because their conscious selves are drains into which the world, including our objectivized being, pours. Each one of us strives to be absolute, to be the only consciousness, because each one of us is a center of free transcendence who cannot tolerate limitation. Sartre's great insight is that when we center ourselves in the practical viewpoint we experience a moment of separation from the world in which we may feel that we are beginning life anew and may make a fresh start. The notion of a new beginning initiated with full awareness lies at the root of Sartre's insistence upon our responsibility for our choices and his antipathy toward those who define us according to laws of physical necessity or final causes. Our dignity, for Sartre, resides in the fact that we make ourselves by giving ourselves our own meanings, that we hurl ourselves into the future. Society is so terrible because it systematically deprives us of our freedom by making us relative to the projects of others, constants and variables within their experiments. Each one of us wills to be the only one who experiments, the only being-for-itself, the only one who expresses the world. The others are terrible and hateful to us because we know that they are as absolute in their freedom as we are but that we can never penetrate their interiority nor they ours. Each is an object to the other and a subject to oneself.

From a vitalistic viewpoint, Sartre's ethic is a continual repetition of the moment of betrayal, at which we separate ourselves from others and resolve to care for, and attend to, ourselves in solitude. But Sartre is far more ruthless and thorough than other practical philosophers because he acknowledges that the essence of control is mere transcendence out of one present and into the next and refuses to justify that transcendence by any partial meaning. Sartre's genius has been to make of the consequence of betrayal the supreme value and to exhort us to deny our concrete duration in favor of negativity and indeterminacy. He dignifies the child's pitiful resolution to go it alone, to "show them," and to resist impositions. Hence, he takes an attitude that emerges out of fear and resentment and enjoins us to make it our goal. Sartre, then, is consumed by *ressentiment,* the experience in which we unconsciously invert our values and preferences, glorifying what we loathe and detracting from what we secretly honor. Sartre's *ressentiment,* however, is more pure than other instances of value inversion, because it does not embroider the motive of control with compensatory meanings but affirms it as it essentially is. Existentialist ethics, which prescribes that we be absolutely responsible for ourselves individually, is the most complete affirmation of death in contemporary Western philosophy. The alternative to it, which flows from an affirmation of life, is loyalty to one another and to our own incomplete, concrete, and polemical being. Such an ethic of sacrifice is based upon responsibility for one another, upon each one defending the other's dignity so that suspicion is lessened and self-defense is less tempting. Dignity here does not reside in freedom but in a concrete center for expressing the world and a unique autobiography out of which particular possibilities grow.

The agony of Sartre's ethics is that we must continually determine ourselves and become objects to ourselves and others, while the agony of an ethics of sacrifice based on appreciation is that we must sacrifice life in order to live. However much we are trusting and loyal, the practical viewpoint demands that we carry forward some expressions into action and suppress others, that we attend to some concerns and neglect others, and that we care for only some of the possibilities and needs even of the concrete beings to whom we are bound most intimately. We must continually choose between ourselves and others and between submitting ourselves to the motive of control and committing ourselves to trust. Awareness of sacrifice provides us with no secure standard by which we can guide our choices among possible objects of care and attention and between separation and attempted union. We live most in accord with our being when we are related to one another by bonds of loyalty, but we cannot count on mutuality and must always hold part of ourselves in reserve in silent anticipation of betrayal or abandonment. The other side of our uniquely concrete being is our stubborn particularity and limitation, the deep imbalance and disharmony created by the surplus of what we can appreciate over what we can attend to and enact in any present. The ethic of sacrifice does not heal the imbalance and reconcile the disharmony but merely invites us to extend as far as possible our appreciation of what we are leaving behind, turning away from, and destroying when we pursue a meaning projected into the symbolic past-present-future. It also tempers and deflates our pretensions by criticizing all of our meanings in terms of life's contradictory ideal of conscious completion, and it alerts us that our object of conduct is not a symbol but particular concrete persons. From the practical viewpoint, which we are destined to take except for brief interludes of appreciation, we cannot evade the motive of control but can only moderate its ruthless exclusivity with the compassion that sustains trust and loyalty and that creates the interior bond between us.

## 3. IN DEFENSE OF OURSELVES

We are remarkable, mysterious, complex, and unstable syntheses of life and awareness, who are polemical in the present, incomplete toward the future, and uniquely concrete toward the past. We spend most of our lives centered in the practical viewpoint, projecting meanings into the symbolic past-present-future and striving to actualize them, but we are fundamentally impractical and are pulled toward a fullness of life, a plenitude, in the expanded and continuous present that melts into the next moment in an unbroken flow. Through fear and betrayal we are bound to the motive of control, which impels us to protect ourselves so that we can vault from one instant to another, but we are also able to suspend control and to appreciate our being and to temper control with compassion through the affirmation of life and the awareness of sacrifice. In order to control ourselves, our circumstances, and others so that we can achieve partial completion, we project an idea of nature in which each event is determined within an endless chain of efficient causes, yet we elude necessity by commenting on our existence through feeling, expression, and compassionate appreciation, all of which still life's insistent drive toward conscious completion and all of which open up a span of attention. From the practical viewpoint each experience is a means to some end that substitutes for and conceals our native and contradictory ideal, but for appreciation and sacrifice we ourselves are the only supreme ends, the fullest realities.

We reach the limit of our knowledge when we attempt to understand how it is possible that life makes a dwelling within itself for awareness. As syntheses of life and awareness we are unable to explain our origins, because any explanations that we offer already presuppose the synthesis. Most thought stops short of mystery and explains us to ourselves by separating one or more aspects of our existence from the others and interpreting them as causes or logical grounds. All such explanations falsify us by diminishing us, even those that insist upon our dignity. Interpretations of our being that define us in terms of physical categories must explain away life, expression, and appreciation; those that define us as forms of animal life must explain away expression and appreciation; and those that define us as cultural or symbolic beings must explain away appreciation. Even the most generous explanations of ourselves—the ones that separate us from other animals by our rationality, symbolization, conventions, tools, or art, by our culture-creating spirit—remain within the practical viewpoint ruled by meaning and never penetrate behind it to the intuition that divides the conventional ego from the fundamental self and reveals the stubborn heterogeneity of life and awareness. All thought that strives to explain ourselves to ourselves rather than limiting itself to description is enslaved to meaning. Yet all meanings are exclusive, none is comprehensive, and each is relative to life's contradictory and indefinable ideal.

The many attempts to explain our life, which constitute the Western tradition of philosophy, commit the cognitive fallacy and are sins against us. They arise from analyses of what we have done, which form only a small portion of what we are. The great religions are far more adequate to our being than scientific theories or rationalist philosophies, but they too sin against us by subordinating us to symbolizations of the powers that create, preserve, and destroy us. We cannot deny, certainly, that we are dependent upon powers that are beyond our control and our rational understanding, but we still sin from pride when we substitute mythic vision or special revelation for analytical thought. Religion is eminently practical, a transcendental economy, as Unamuno called it, in which we barter, bargain, and placate to achieve salvation, reconciliation, union, or peace. It negates itself if it preaches disquiet, frustration, conflict, and tragedy. The goal of religion is to justify the solitude that follows from fear and betrayal by embroidering the practical viewpoint with meanings and assuring us that the vast powers that contain and form us are not indifferent to our destiny. Religion, at least, touches mystery, but it strives to pass beyond it. In such striving it compromises with, and succumbs to, our temptation of ourselves to accept symbolic completion as a substitute for concrete and lived fulfillment. A philosophy in which we open ourselves to ourselves makes no judgment about our origins and destiny, noting only that we do not create ourselves and holding all metaphysical and religious visions to be equally possible, including that most terrifying vision in which there is, indeed, an absolute being, but an absurd absolute indifferent entirely to us except as we are means to its own realization. We are, as the Buddhists have shown, capable even of finding peace by courting the void; but we seem unwilling or unable to affirm a reality in which an absolute creates us, uses us up, and then ruthlessly discards us with no care for our feelings or desires. Yet such an absolute would merely be treating us, on a grand scale, the way we usually treat one another. We might in fact meditate upon whether a will to believe in the absurd absolute is not the most effective way for us to highlight and intensify the infinite worth of our finite existence. Were we to affirm the absurd absolute we would not be rebels against the absurd or loyal citizens of the absolute community but renegades who bite the hand that has fed us but will also strike us down.

The culmination of a tragic vision of life is the image of the renegade, the apostate, who accepts no symbolic consolation for life's frustration but is aware as possible of the sacrifices involved in any action. The renegade is one who has gone back to the origins of the practical viewpoint, has passed through the withering nothingness of pure attention, has reenacted the moment of betrayal, and has yet affirmed life despite its contradiction and frustration. Those who affirm life are renegades and not partisans because they must continually resist not only the threats and promises of others who seek to mobilize them in the service of meanings but also the temptation that comes from within themselves to separate themselves from others and to justify themselves by pursuing a meaning of their own, whether it masquerades as service to a cause or an idol, or whether it is merely the desperate quest for autonomy and independence. Affirmation of life, then, is not possible except in reaction against the resentful tendencies that we all carry forward and that plunge us into suspicion and mistrust, keeping us from risking loyalty to unique and concrete others.

The renegade attempts to encounter others in their terrifying and surprising reality, not to avoid them by interposing fictions between direct relations. Yet renegades also know that we are destined to the practical viewpoint and must create a conventional ego that divides us from one another and from ourselves. Renegades, then, are compassionate over our tragedy and incompletion and appreciative of our uniqueness, but they are ruthless with regard to our practical fate. The renegade's virtue is ruthless compassion, which combines awareness of sacrifice with willingness to make sacrifices both of others and of oneself.

Renegades walk a tightrope between expression of their own unique being and expression of others to themselves. They vacillate between honesty and mendacity, sometimes making themselves vulnerable by according trust and at other times raising their defenses when they believe that loyalty would be the equivalent of death. Yet they try to ready themselves for a moment in which they may choose to die so that other lives will be enhanced. Renegades are aware that they harm others and violate themselves many times each day, if only because their span of attention is limited by the dispersion and fragility of life. Each choice is a sacrifice involving its own implicit obligation, but because renegades lack an objective standard of conduct they cannot help but experience guilt for having suppressed some goods. Guilt becomes most acute when it involves a breach of trust, a withdrawal of care and attention from others to whom one has pledged loyalty. Such guilt can become so intolerable that it is falsified and expressed as resentment against the others for their supposedly unwarranted demands. Yet resentment only compounds guilt, providing it with a new occasion. For the renegade there is no escape from guilt because all acts of atonement are merely symbolic and do not repair the harm done to the other's concrete being. Renegades cannot save themselves from guilt but can be saved only by the others through their forgiveness.

The renegade's guilt is not rational, because if we must always sacrifice in any event we might just as well try to suppress the past and turn our attention to our future conduct. Yet not to feel guilt is to separate ourselves from the others, to break our bonds with them by losing sight of what we have done to them; in brief, to withdraw our attention from them and betray them. Christianity has acknowledged the guilt that we all carry into the practical viewpoint because of our betrayals, but it promises that our sins can be redeemed through faith. Opponents of Christianity have, for the most part, rejected guilt along with redemption, tempting us with the promise that if we renounce faith we will be able to make our own rules more in accord with our desires and limitations and therefore suffer guilt no longer. The renegade, however, attempts neither to summon up faith in redemption nor to overcome guilt. If we are redeemed at all, it is by forgiving one another, because only forgiveness makes loyalty durable. Regret, which often seems so close to guilt, and desperate efforts to atone symbolically are defensive measures aimed at showing the others that one is still worthy of their trust and loyalty. We cannot help but regret and atone, because we cannot help but fear. Yet we wish deeply that we could just be forgiven. Renegades struggle to forgive others and wait silently to be forgiven. The struggling and the waiting never cease and must be continually repeated because the essence of our life is to sacrifice ourselves and one another.

The renegade is satisfied with nothing less than the impossible, the conscious completion of life. Any concession or compromise that blunts life's native ideal is, for the renegade, a diminution of ourselves, a denial of our hunger for fullness and plenitude, and most important, a prior and calculated rejection of the other person's unique and concrete reality. Renegades have turned away from and against partisanship because they have appreciated that we ourselves—each one of us in our particularity, fragility, transiency, and finitude—are the effective reality, richer and more worthy than any idea or possibility. Each one of us is a finite being who is infinitely precious and who we may seek to express to ourselves and therefore to save from solitude. Yet each one of us is also a self separated from others by fear and betrayal who we must coerce, bribe, flatter, and manipulate so that we can be assured of care and attention. Not even the renegade can resolve our polemical being.

Philosophical renegades and apostates do not, any more than do their political and clerical counterparts, choose to pursue practical success. A successful life demands adherence to a symbolized cause, to a ruthless trimming away of appreciation, to the principle that knowledge is virtue. Renegades are actuated by the intuitive knowledge that we are fundamentally impractical beings who are destined to action, and this knowledge provides no standard for conduct but only a sense of its tragedy and of our dignity.

# AFTERWORD

We live in a period, the second half of the twentieth century, in which philosophy does not belong to independent, critical, and venturesome individuals who go forth, as Josiah Royce urged, into the wilderness of consciousness and return to our everyday life with inspiring visions of our possibilities. The last generation of great philosophers who took personal responsibility for showing us the contours of our life, the existentialists, has few surviving members. For the generations born after World War I philosophy became and still remains a specialized academic discipline devoted to analyzing symbolic communication or a servant of nineteenth-century ideologies or traditional systems of religious belief. Lulled by the hermetic discourse of dying schools, intimidated by the arcane symbolism of formal logicians, disenchanted with the tediously brutal and repetitious slogans of ideologues, and bored by the histrionics of extremist cults, we tend to forget the rich and variegated intellectual life at the turn of our century. We still draw whatever élan we can muster from the work of such great spirits as William James, Nietzsche, Wilhelm Dilthey, Husserl, Freud, and Bergson, but we borrow their concepts and do not follow their examples. It is almost as though we believe that the last creative words have been said or, even more ominously, that creative words (words that evoke and shape a freshly personal vision of life) are too dangerous and threatening to speak.

There are many reasons that philosophers have retreated from the challenge of speaking to our life as a whole, a challenge that is renewed in each generation by our life's continual mutation. Our existence has become more collectivized; as Heidegger noted, we live in the age of the "we," not of the "I." Whenever institutions become more important to us than we are to ourselves, philosophers band together into self-protective guilds or attempt to win approval or relieve their guilt by allowing official definitions of the situation to become their first premises. Whether philosophy is a means of escape or of gaining relevance, individual thinkers must justify themselves by appealing to tribal gods (Karl Marx, Freud, Thomas Aquinas, Husserl) or to objectified discourses. Personal responsibility and unique visions are rejected, and obedience and doctrinal purity are sought. In a collectivized world, philosophy is on the defensive and is often a response to fear and a hunger for security. That there is abundant reason to be afraid and to think defensively does not change the fact that we have lost something vital.

We are still not fully aware of the loss or even of what has been lost. Heidegger only recently died, and at this writing Sartre is still alive. But who will take their place? We are witnessing the death of an idea of philosophy that is profoundly significant to our civilization. Philosophers are committed to the search for truth, but the ways in which truth is achieved are various. Today we seem to believe that truth is only objective and should be sought by working over and cleaning up existing texts, whether those texts be great books, ancient myths, or our ordinary discourse. We have nearly no tolerance for our own experience but are capable of assimilating only mediated experiences that have been detoxified for us by others. Philosophy has become a vaccine against life, made safe by the legitimating purification of traditions and schools. Of course, someone had to create the text out of a venture into the wilderness, but this risky and disorderly enterprise is forgotten by contemporary thinkers who are dedicated to perpetuating culture rather than renewing it. We do not interpret our lives but interpret interpretations of them. We have lost the confidence to interpret on our own accounts and are losing the idea that such fresh interpretation is even possible. The alternative to specious objectification is the notion that truth about our existence is not achieved by a consensus of professional opinion but through the clash and congruity of personalized visions. No personalized vision, even the most disciplined and reflective, will be entirely adequate to any other human being; but each one will be able to enrich and broaden the lives of others, showing them what they have neglected, revealing what they have been afraid to express to themselves, perhaps confirming them in truths they have glimpsed but have not uttered. The quest for consensus has not led to unity but to hermetic retreat, ideological warfare, superficial relativism, and most important, to the failure to appreciate. The idea of philosophy that we are losing is that each thinker must strive for universality while remaining aware of partiality. Today we do our partial work in the intellectual division of labor, borrowing our universals from the dead.

I am, of course, not exempt from my own indictment.

While I have attempted adventures into the wilderness, enough of the humility (or is it anxiety?) of the age remains with me to impel me to acknowledge my debts and influences and to place myself in a personal tradition compounded of the works that have influenced my thought. Preceding thinkers have helped to shape the very conception of this work, its underlying ontology, and its moral attitude. The following brief remarks are meant to acknowledge them.

The design of this work, the idea of examining the interrelated motives of our life, first occurred to me when I read George Santayana's *Reason in Society* more than a decade ago. Santayana was part of the movement in philosophy at the turn of the century that rejected historicism and sought to define human universals derived from scrutiny of the dimensions of our experience. He was a relativist in the sense that he defined progress in relation to the achievement of cultural ideals but rejected the notion that the ideals of some cultures are more advanced than those of others. Within any culture, however, Santayana believed that there are universal forms or orders of social life, which he called natural society, free society, and ideal society. By natural society Santayana meant those relations in which the person's attention is fixed upon the fortunes of particular natural and corporate bodies. It is rooted in the love for human beings on whom the individual depends for sustenance and is fulfilled in experienced and material solidarity. Free society is friendship among persons transcending material need; ideal society is common participation in symbolic meanings.

Santayana's orders of social life bear little resemblance to the motives of control, appreciation, and sacrifice that structure the present work, but the idea that orders of social experience cut across substantive cultural diversity informs the design of this project. Santayana was inspired by the Greek tradition and believed that knowledge is virtue. Therefore, the capstone of his social philosophy was ideal society:

> It is an inspiring thought and a true one, that in proportion as a man's interests become humane and his efforts rational, he appropriates and expands a common life, which reappears in all individuals who reach the same impersonal level of ideas—a level which his own influence may help them to maintain.[1]

The themes of tragedy, sacrifice, and incompletion in the present work run against Santayana's hope for a civilized humanism in which we find our fulfillment on the "impersonal level of ideas," in which we are linked, not by trust and loyalty, but by common symbolic attachments. In fact, the present work is very nearly a polemic against Santayana's views, although he was the first philosopher I read systematically and I continue his project of analyzing our life critically.

Far closer to the design of this work is a book written by Santayana's contemporary, the Mexican philosopher Antonio Caso. Caso's *Existence as Economy, as Disinterest, and as Charity*, though little known by English-speaking philosophers, is one of the classics of Mexican thought.[2] Like Santayana, Caso rejected historicism and attempted to define what he called our fundamental "attitudes toward existence." Caso's attitudes are much the same as what I have termed "motives"—they are the forms that coordinate our life. For Caso the principle of life is economy, defined by the formula, "maximum advantage with minimum effort." According to him, all organisms strive to monopolize their environment, but only human beings can transcend the principle of life through disinterest (intuition of unique objects as they are and not as we might use them to our advantage) and through charity (maximum effort with minimum advantage or the complete and active commitment of the individual to others).

Caso's categories have had a deep influence on my thinking, but I have altered them significantly. First, although the motive of control is similar to the attitude of economy, I do not identify control with life but interpret it as a synthesis of life and awareness. Thus, I do not argue that appreciation and sacrifice are "antivital" as Caso held that disinterest and charity are. Second, I do not believe that control is identified with economic maximization, appreciation with pure contemplation, or sacrifice with the antithesis of instrumental reason. Caso's mistake was to define our fundamental attitudes toward existence in terms of ideal principles instead of paying close attention to the ebb and flow of our experience. Although he did not hold that knowledge is virtue and argued that a charitable act is worth more than all of the books of philosophy, Caso did not escape the Greek tradition. He superimposed over our experience concepts that represent idealizations of what we undergo. Economy is a sophisticated rationalization of control, substituting instrumental reason for the impulsion to carry oneself into the next present; disinterest is a sublimation of passionate appreciation; and charity is idealized sacrifice purified of its tragic ambiguity. Caso came closer than any other philosopher I have studied to an adequate design for a philosophy of life, but he would not or could not surrender the quest for clear and distinct, although false, ideas.

Other thinkers, also of the same turn-of-the-century vintage, influenced not so much the design as the content of some of the ideas in this work. The concept of life, defined intuitively and not biologically, originates, of course, in the thought of Henri Bergson.[3] For more than a decade I strove first to understand and then to re-create Bergson's intuition of the *durée*, the unbroken flow of compounding experience. I was sustained by a trust, the only kind of trust befitting a philosopher, that Bergson had actually experienced something that others, who had criticized him, had not tried or had failed to capture. For a long time my efforts were in vain. I could not escape from the grip of what Bergson called the conventional ego, which requires that all experience be interpreted in terms of the symbolic past-present-future. Finally, I experienced a detachment of convention from the rest of my experience and intuited the *durée*. Yet my intuition was not exactly the same as Bergson's, or at least my interpretation of it had a different emphasis. Bergson was concerned with reviving the absolute by placing it in the realm of life rather than in that of thought. Thus, he tended, like Caso, to make idealized and sharp distinctions between orders of experience, in this case between lived and spatialized modes of time. The fundamental self could not be expressed; it was heterogeneous; and it was pure quality. The conventional ego was thoroughly social and linguistic; it was homogeneous; and it was expressed in terms of quantity. I found that the root of the fundamental self was the expression of life's qualitative flow in gesture and vocalization, that language is not altogether social, and that the origin of the conventional ego is self-control in response to fear. Thus, I did not attempt to formulate a metaphysical dualism but tried to stay close to what I experienced: different syntheses of life and awareness. I could not identify the fundamental self with quality, heterogeneity, and privacy, and the conventional ego with quantity, homogeneity, and publicity. The fundamental self was indeed in polemical conflict with the conventional ego, but neither one was a primary metaphysical entity. Both were already syntheses of other realities, life and awareness, which could be only inferred. So, while following Bergson's intuitive lead, I did not travel with him toward the absolute but stayed within the bounds of our stubborn sociality.

A second but much less formidable influence on the polarity of life and awareness was Josiah Royce. Royce of course was an absolute idealist, whose notion that our life is completed by a superhuman being is utterly antithetical to the idea of our incomplete being that plays so great a role in this work.[4] Yet it was Royce who first made me aware that the lived present is created by a span of attention that halts the ceaseless flux of life. His use of this insight to indicate the existence of an absolute and eternal span of attention is neither different in form nor any more critically legitimate than Bergson's use of intuition to indicate the metaphysical priority of the vital impetus. When the scaffolding of the absolute is removed from Royce's thought, what remains is very similar to many aspects of the present work. Royce held that we are each uniquely concrete beings and that we can never know how we are completed, although he refused to leave us incomplete. His metaphysics blinded him to our polemical being, but he did oppose to the scientific vision of nature ("the world of description") a vision of social reality ("the world of appreciation"). Royce, in fact, is the only philosopher I have encountered who acknowledges appreciation to be a fundamental category of our existence. His ideal was that we be "sensitive appreciators of life," and he believed that our vocation was not to serve an abstract ideal (Santayana's community of impersonal ideas) but to complete one another's meanings.

A third significant influence on the polarity of life and awareness is José Vasconcelos, who along with Caso initiated the golden age of Mexican philosophy at the turn of the century. Vasconcelos who, like Bergson, employed an intuitive method, argued that consciousness is a spontaneous coordination of heterogeneous contents according to motives or ends. He contrasted "constructive philosophy," which describes the contours of concrete experience, with "reductive philosophy," which abstracts from the concrete and reconceives it in terms of an idea.[5] Vasconcelos also thirsted for the absolute and believed that reality is an aesthetic totality principled by plenitude and pleasure. His contribution to my thought has been the idea that our experience is a synthesis of heterogeneous contents—life and awareness.

A third group of thinkers, perhaps the most important, has been decisive in shaping or at least corroborating my moral sensibility. William James; Miguel de Unamuno; and their Uruguayan contemporary, Carlos Vaz Ferreira, are distinguished from other turn-of-the-century and later philosophers by their embracement of a plenitude of experience and their acute awareness of the sacrifice of value involved in action. James is the most generous of North American philosophers and also the one who stayed closest to experience as it is lived. The guiding concern of James's work, which underlies and informs his radical empiricism and his hypothesis of a pluralistic universe, is moral. At the root of his attitude toward life is the distinction between those who live defensively and "intrench" themselves by "retraction" from the region of what they cannot securely possess, and those who live expansively and inclusively, seeking to sympathize with others and to enrich their own experience. According to James, the sympathetic person may often be uncertain about individual self-definition (the conventional ego), but the spread of the self's content "more than atones for this." [6] The great problem with James's defense of sympathetic appreciation is his failure to think deeply about the reasons that so many people intrench and retract themselves. He was an admirable philosophical psychologist, but he stopped short of a philosophical psychiatry that might have taught him how we violate, wound, and betray one another. Thus, he is lacking in a sense of tragedy that tempers and renders ambiguous the struggle to appreciate. James believed that it was possible not only to sympathize but to live a sympathetic life. His optimism betrays a belief that knowledge is virtue, that were we to understand the worth of living inclusively we would be less concerned with the maintenance and perpetuation of our discrete and conventional identities.

Miguel de Unamuno cannot be accused of slighting tragedy. From his *Tragic Sense of Life* I learned one of the basic ideas in the present work: there is a native ideal immanent to life, and that ideal is life's conscious completion of itself.[7] Unamuno was an agonist and a philosopher of paradox because he understood better than anyone else that our life is contradictory. We demand, as he put it, "all or nothing."

We will to be "ourselves and everyone else." We are inevitably disappointed, and therein lies our tragedy. Unamuno understood our polemical being when he pitted the "individual" (the intrenched and retracted self) against the "person" (the expansive and inclusive self), locating the conflict within each one of us rather than dispersing it into distinct personality types. He grasped our uniquely concrete being when he characterized each one of us as a unique species incorporating many selves and when he based his thought upon the substantial "man of flesh and bone." But above all Unamuno was the philosopher of our incomplete being, urging us to acknowledge our thirst for plenitude and hunger for immortality, and to struggle against the substitution of symbolic meanings for life. Unamuno affirmed life more fully than any other thinker I have encountered. When he plunged to the "bottom of the abyss" he was tempted by suicide, but he overcame the temptation simply by willing to live. He never justified his affirmation as Camus attempted to do in *The Myth of Sisyphus*, because that would have meant making meaning a substitute for living.

Carlos Vaz Ferreira, who corresponded with Unamuno, performed the same role of initiating independent and critical philosophy in Uruguay that Caso and Vasconcelos performed in Mexico. As generous as James and Unamuno, Vaz Ferreira was primarily an epistemologist who contrasted systematic thinking with skeptical and creative thinking:

> There are two ways of making use of an exact observation or a just reflection: the first is to draw from it, consciously or unconsciously, a *system* meant to be applied to every case; the second is to reserve it, elaborate on it, consciously or unconsciously also, as some-

thing to take into account when one reflects on real and concrete problems in particular cases.[8]

Vaz Ferreira believed that our life is multidimensional and has so many loose ends and heterogeneous ideals that it can never be described adequately by a system of principles. He carried over his defense of skeptical and creative thinking into his ethical theory, arguing that the goal of ethics "is not to arrive at a school, but at a *state of spirit.*"[9] His spirit was to live "without anesthesia," without religious faith, ultimate meaning, or hope in the achievement of our ideals. Yet living without anesthesia also meant living in the awareness and appreciation of many ideals, conscious always of the sacrifices that we make.

There have of course been many other influences on the ideas in this work. The Russians, Dostoevski and Lev Shestov, both of whom challenged the principle that knowledge is virtue; the Germans, Kant, Max Stirner, Nietzsche, and Martin Heidegger, who were ruthlessly critical of dogma; the neglected North Americans, Elijah Jordan and David Swenson, who insisted upon our tragic existence in a culture hostile to their insight; the Argentinian Alejandro Korn and the Peruvian Alejandro Deústua, who refined many of Bergson's observations—all of them have provided me with cause to explore my life further under their guidance. But none of their influences was as direct, lasting, and comprehensive as those of the eight thinkers previously discussed.

Despite the many influences I acknowledge (and there are a great many more than I have listed), my own vision is not a collage of their ideas but the result of taking their insights and attempting to re-create them in my life, and of challenging them with my own intuitions. I have tried to stay as close as possible to my experience, elaborating on it, as Vaz Ferreira suggested, and not systematizing it. I have tried to express other thinkers to myself and to enrich my life and thus to make it more representative. Basic to my vision, however, is a guiding theme that, though it may not be original, is at least fresh in emphasis. We are impractical beings whose most profound vocation is to express one another to ourselves. Yet we betray one another and are impelled to become practical by creating separate selves. No knowledge, whether it is rational, revealed, intuitive, or empirical, can heal our divided and incomplete being. We are irremediably social and uniquely concrete. We seek a plenitude of life but are inevitably sacrifices. We are tragic figures.

# NOTES

1. George Santayana, *Reason in Society* (New York: The Macmillan Company, Collier Books, 1962), p. 149. See also my commentaries: "Santayana: Conservative or Philosopher of Reason?" *Modern Age* 13 (Winter 1968–69): 51–61. *Philosophy, Theory, and Method in Contemporary Political Thought* (Glenview, Ill.: Scott, Foresman and Company, 1971), pp. 83–90.

2. Antonio Caso, *La Existencia Como Economía, Como Desinterés y Como Caridad* (México: Ediciones de la Secretaria de Educación Pública, 1943). See also my commentary: *The Polarity of Mexican Thought: Instrumentalism and Finalism* (University Park: The Pennsylvania State University Press, 1976), pp. 31–44.

3. Henri Bergson, *Time and Free Will* (New York: Harper & Row, Harper Torchbooks, 1960). See also my reworking of Bergson's intuition: *Meaning and Appreciation: Time and Modern Political Life* (West Lafayette, Ind.: Purdue University Press, 1977).

4. Josiah Royce, *The World and the Individual*, vol. 2 (New York: Dover Publications, 1959). See also my commentary with Deena Weinstein: "Josiah Royce's Idealist Sociology of Knowledge," *Social Science* 49 (Autumn 1974): 213–219.

5. José Vasconcelos, *Obras Completas*, tomo IV (México: Libreros Mexicanos Unidos, 1961). See also my commentaries: *The Polarity of Mexican Thought*, pp. 16–30, and "The Structure of Anti-Positivist Philosophy in Latin America," *Humanitas* 16 (1975): 174–177.

6. William James, *The Principles of Psychology*, vol. 1 (New York: Dover Publications, 1950), p. 313. See also my commentaries: *Philosophy, Theory, and Method*, pp. 32–34, and "Life and Politics as Plural: James and Bentley on the Twentieth-Century Problem," *Journal of Value Inquiry* 5 (Winter 1971): 282–291.

7. Miguel de Unamuno, *The Tragic Sense of Life* (New York: Dover Publications, 1954). See also my commentary: "Unamuno and the Agonies of Modernization," *Review of Politics* 38 (January 1976): 40–56.

8. Carlos Vaz Ferreira, *Estudios Filosóficos* (Buenos Aires: Aguilar, 1961), p. 160. See also my commentary: "The Structure of Anti-Positivist Philosophy," *Humanitas* 16: 177–180.

9. Vaz Ferreira, *Estudios Filosóficos*, p. 36.

# INDEX OF NAMES

# INDEX OF TOPICS